Piano Book Series

Book 1: Beginner

1st Edition

Created by James Atin-Godden
Illustration and design by Meredith Wolting
Notated by James Atin-Godden
Notated with MuseScore

Music and Lyrics by
James Atin-Godden and Aniqa Qadir

To hear audio examples of all of the music in this series, go to:
https://soundcloud.com/jamesagmusic/albums

Thank you to my students who helped me believe in this thing.

Thank you to Aniqa, who was my most important consultant and helped with every part of this.

Thank you to Meredith for putting so much inspiration and dedication into this and making it beautiful.

Thank you to my amazing and supportive parents.

On the Methodology

This is a book for piano students with a teacher. It is intended for slightly older piano students aged 7+, but younger kids could enjoy it too!

From a teaching perspective, The A-G Piano Book Series is written with the intention of decluttering music education. Every teacher has their own way of doing things and every student requires a unique approach to teaching. This book aims to provide instructional material and fun songs for students to play and learn from. The music has been written to be educational, but rooted in contemporary aesthetics. It's less classical, and more like the music from movies and video games.

This book is designed within a principal of minimalism. There are no teacher duet parts or long explanations of concepts. The music is designed to be more accessible to students who learn by ear and by pattern-recognition. When I was a piano student, I always struggled with reading but I excelled at pieces where I could identify chord structures or patterns and then could just memorize it. I believe other students are like this too. This book is for them.

In relation to a lot of other method books, the right hand has more shifting and more difficult fingerings, while the left hand is much simpler. Deeper into the series, fingering is often left up to interpretation. The whole series is structured a little bit like a video game. It gets a lot of the tutorials out of the way early on, and then focuses on teaching through experiential learning.

Please don’t take this music too seriously! Change notes, add your own flare, play at your own pace, and just have fun!

- James Atin-Godden

Spell these words on the piano.

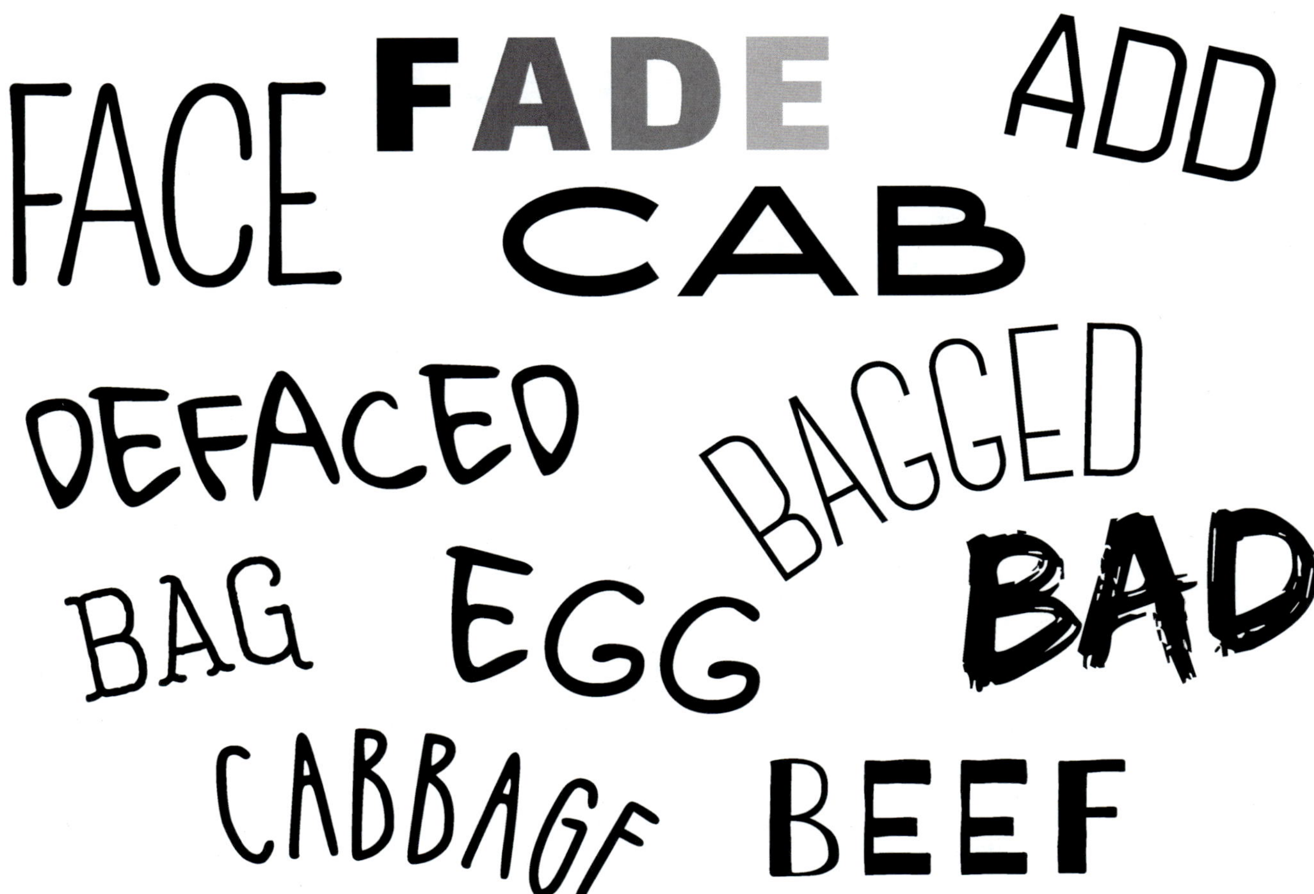

Now, play these songs! For now, don't worry about what fingers you use. Just hit the right notes and try to copy the timing of these songs. I think you might know them!

Twinkle Twinkle Little Star

C C G G A A G	F F E E D D C
Twin kle Twin kle Lit tle Star,	how I won der what you are.

G G F F E E D	G G F F E E D
Up a bove the world so high,	like a dia mond in the sky.

C C G G A A G	F F E E D D C
Twin kle Twin kle Lit tle Star,	how I won der what you are.

Row, Row, Row your Boat

C C C D E E D E F G

Row, row, row your boat gen tly down the stream.

C C C G G G E E E C C C

Mer ri ly mer ri ly mer ri ly mer ri ly

G F E D C

Life is but a dream.

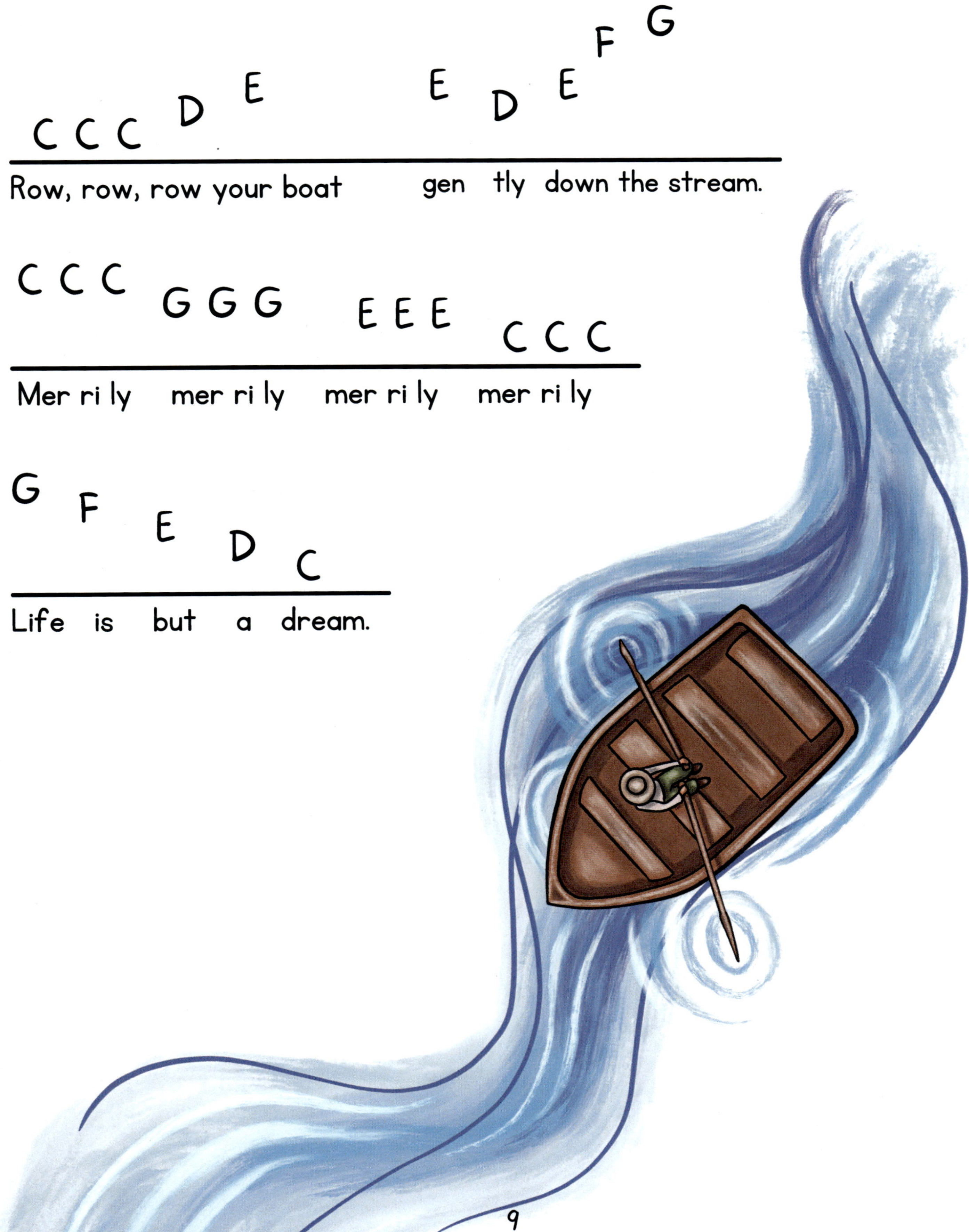

Happy Birthday

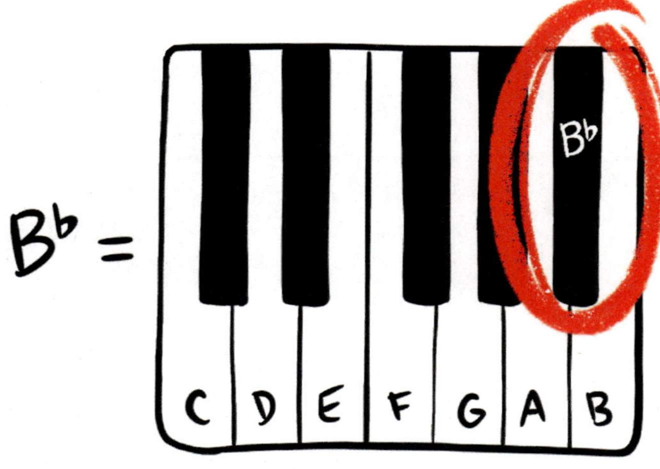

C C D C F E

Happy Birthday to you

C C D C G F

Happy Birthday to you

C C C A F E D

Happy Birthday dear student

B♭ B♭ A F G F

Happy Birthday to you.

Finger Numbers

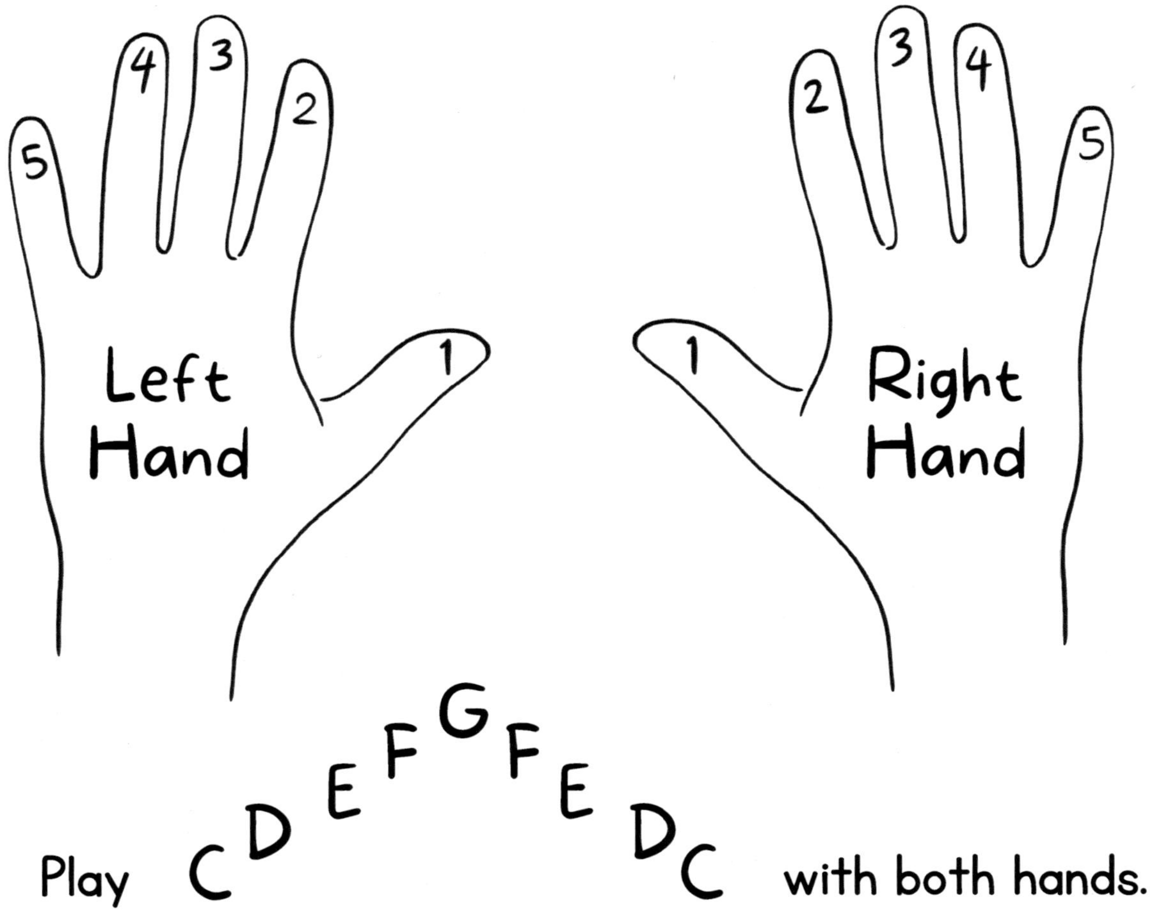

Play C D E F G F E D C with both hands.

Left hand will start with pinky and go

5 4 3 2 1 2 3 4 5

Right hand will start with thumb and go

1 2 3 4 5 4 3 2 1

Counting Basics

quarter note = 1 beat

half note = 2 beats

whole note = 4 beats

Practice:

Clap these.

Mary Had A Little Lamb

Play this song with each hand in C position.
First play with right hand, and then try left hand.

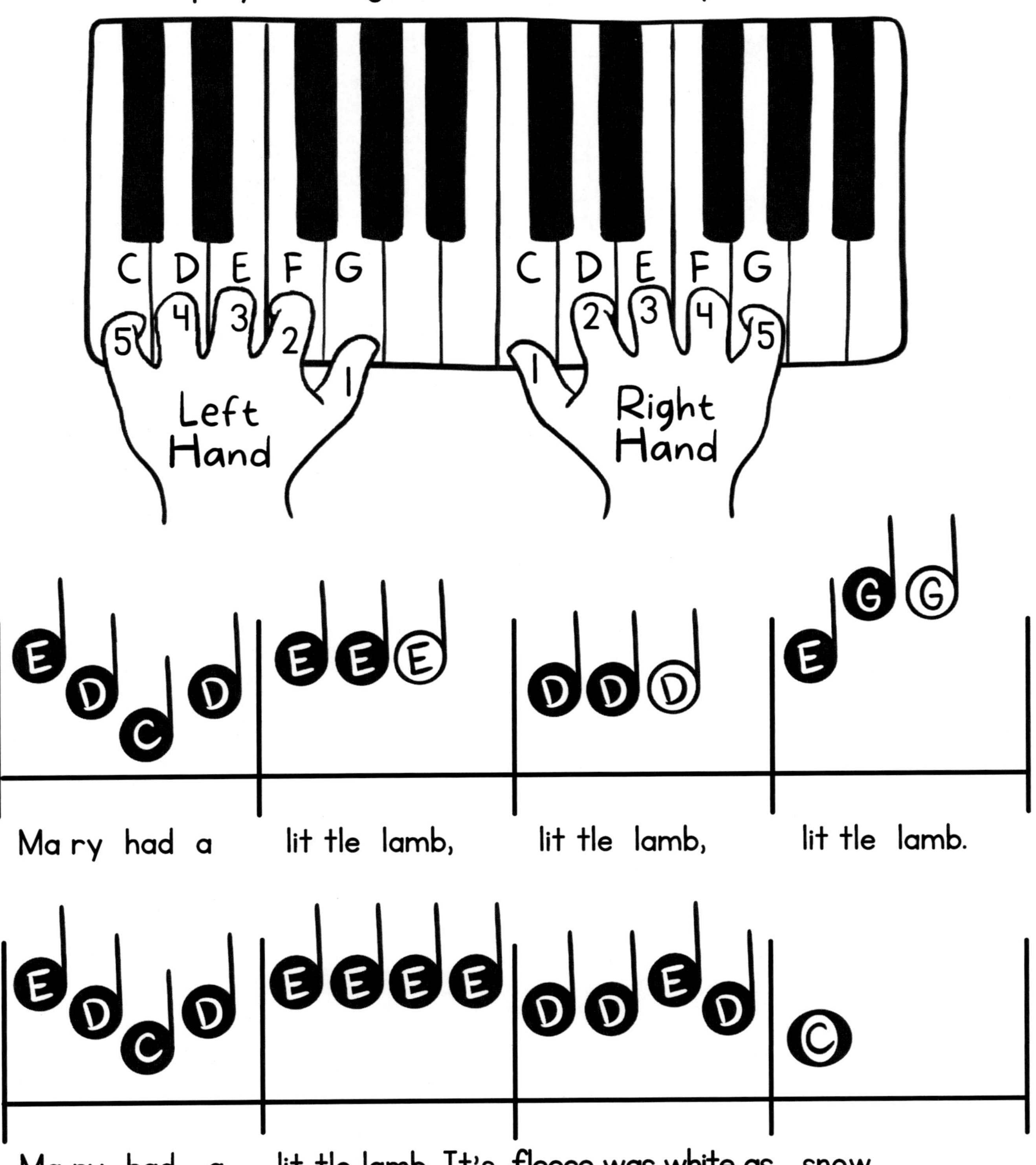

Jingle Bells

Play this song with each hand in C position.
First play with right hand, and then try left hand.

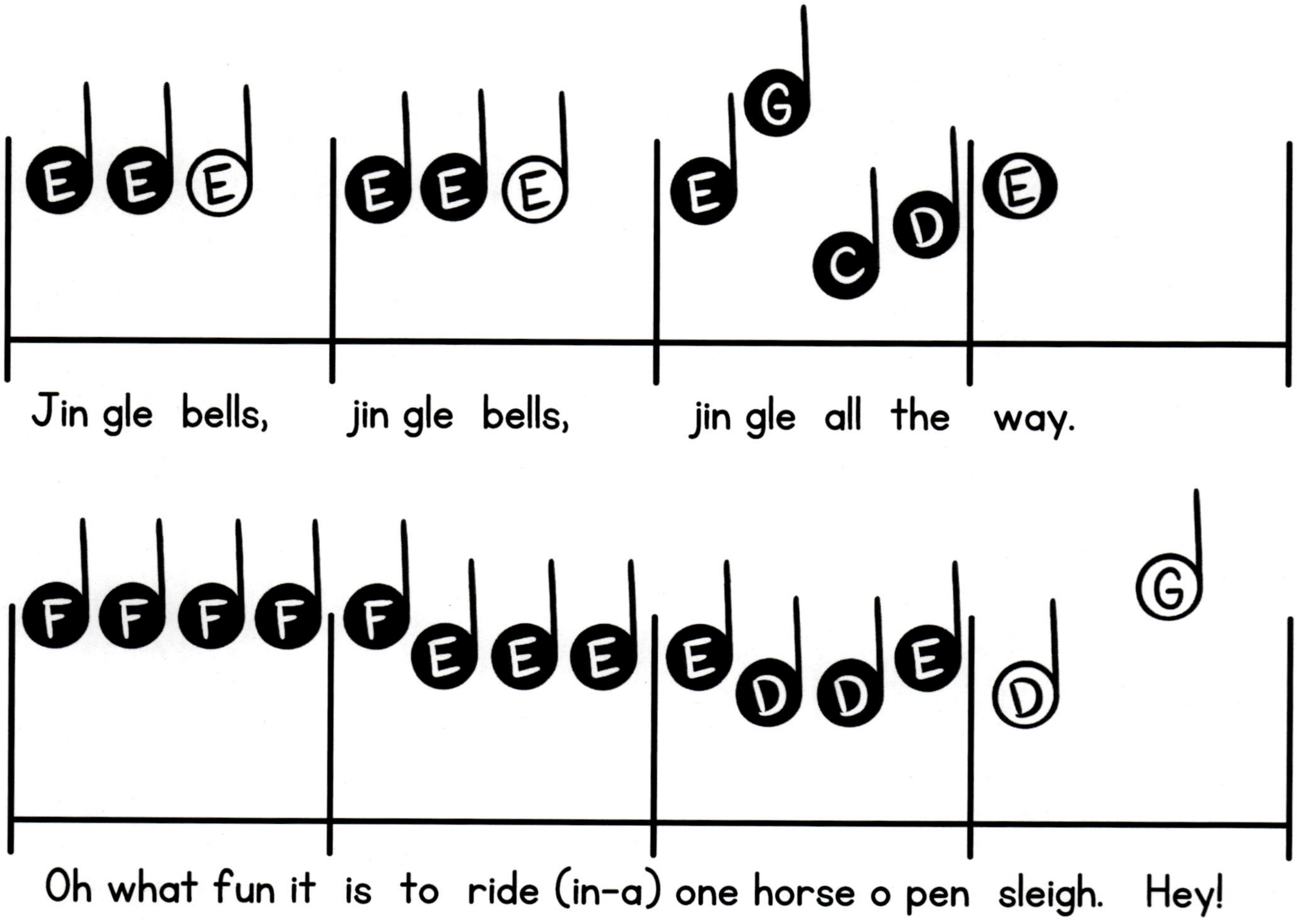

E E E | E E E | E G C D | E

Jin gle bells, jin gle bells, jin gle all the way.

F F F F | F E E E | E D D E | D G

Oh what fun it is to ride (in-a) one horse o pen sleigh. Hey!

Yankee Doodle

Play this song with your right hand in C position. Put your left hand beside it with your left thumb on B.

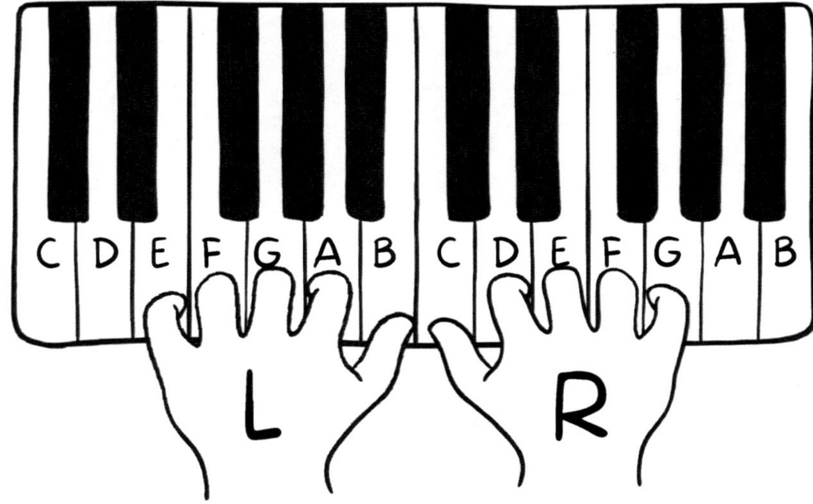

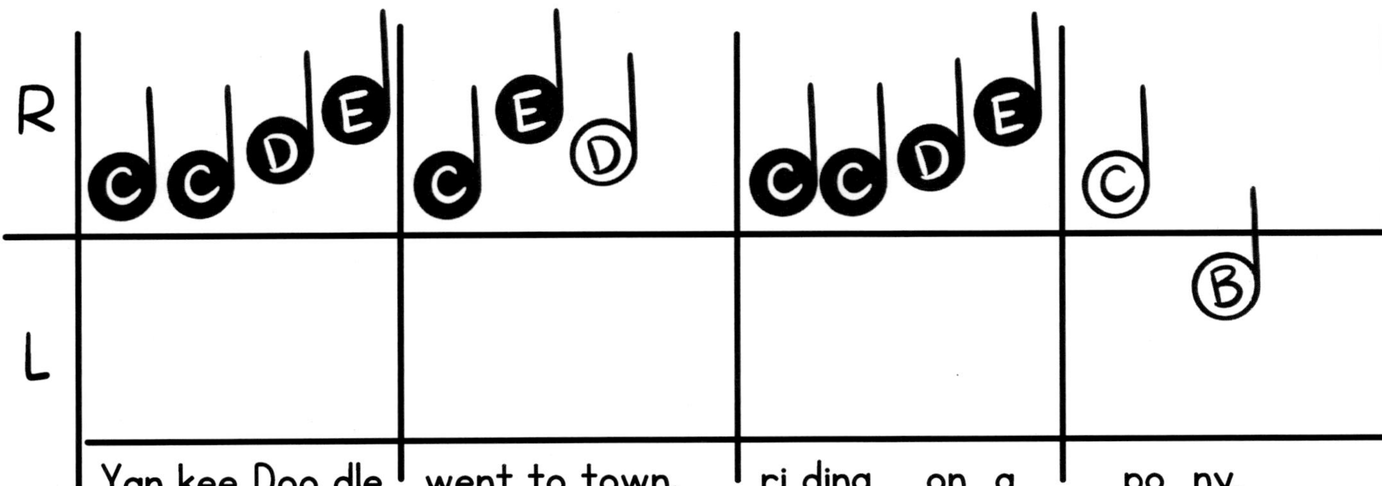

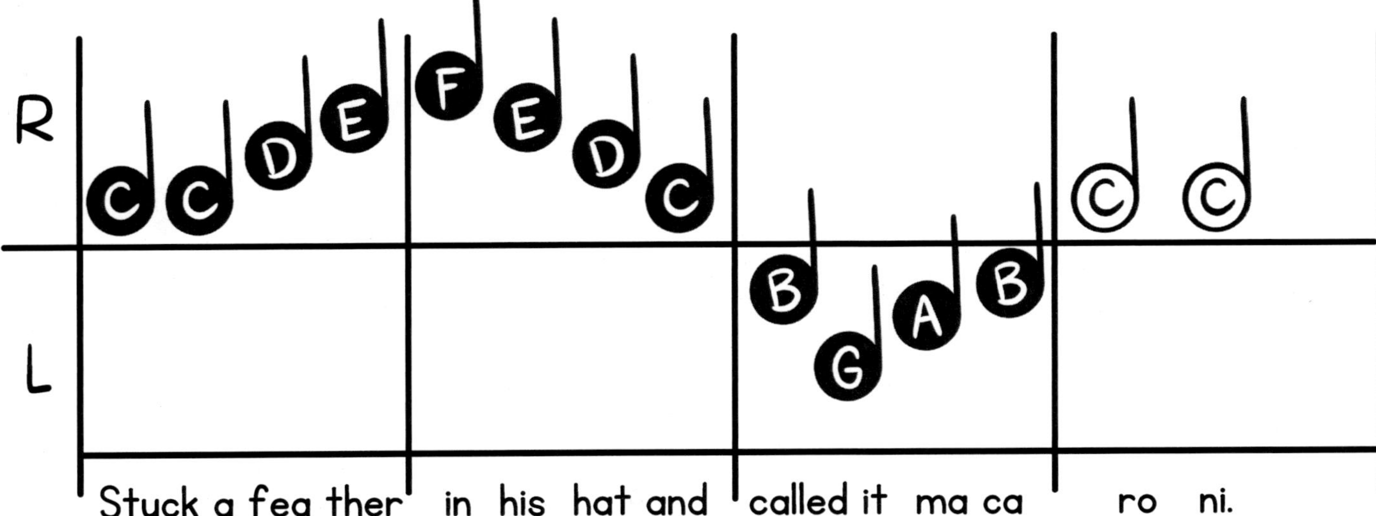

The Grand Staff

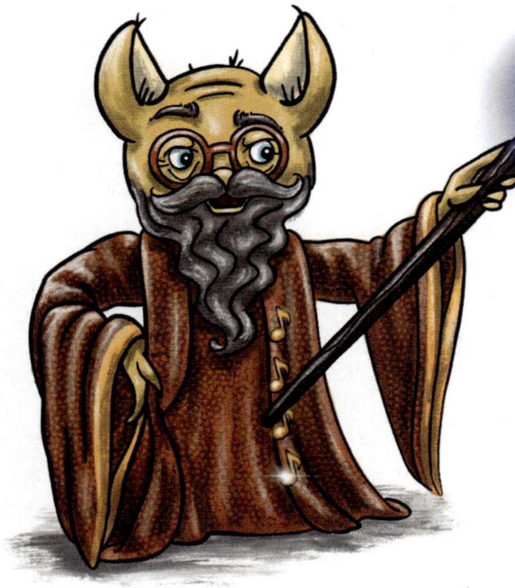

This is called the Grand Staff.
It's how we read music.

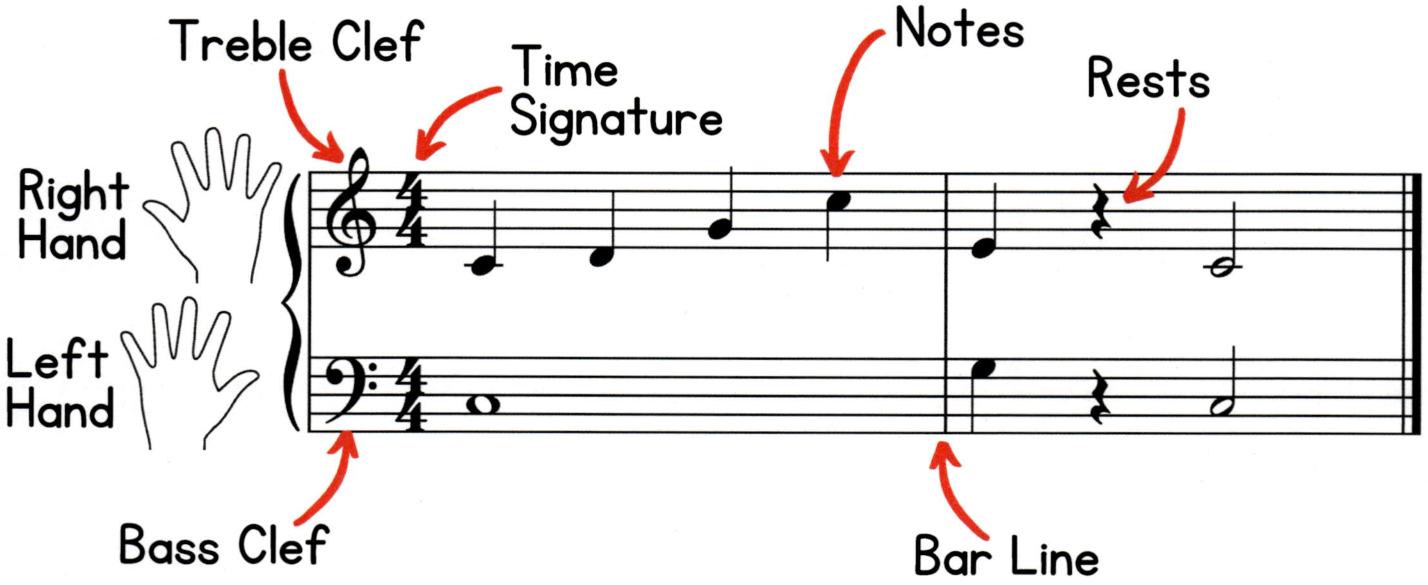

Treble Clef
Time Signature
Notes
Rests
Right Hand
Left Hand
Bass Clef
Bar Line

Kinds of Notes and Rests

quarter note 1 beat

half note 2 beats

dotted half note 3 beats

whole note 4 beats

quarter rest 1 beat

half rest 2 beats

whole rest 4 beats

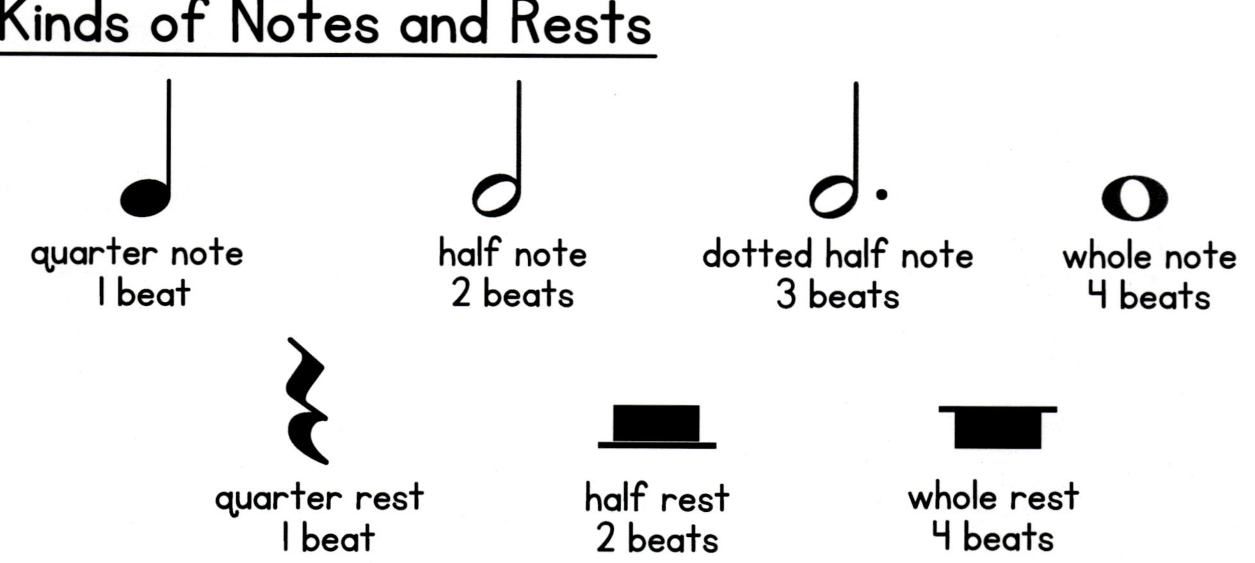

This is called the Time Signature. It tells you how many beats are in each bar. For now, let's look at the top number. This says there are 4 beats in every bar.

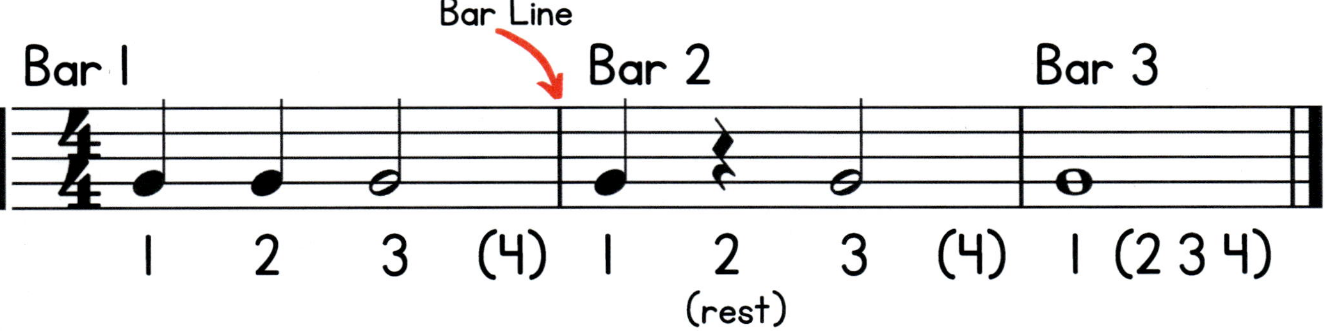

Practice:

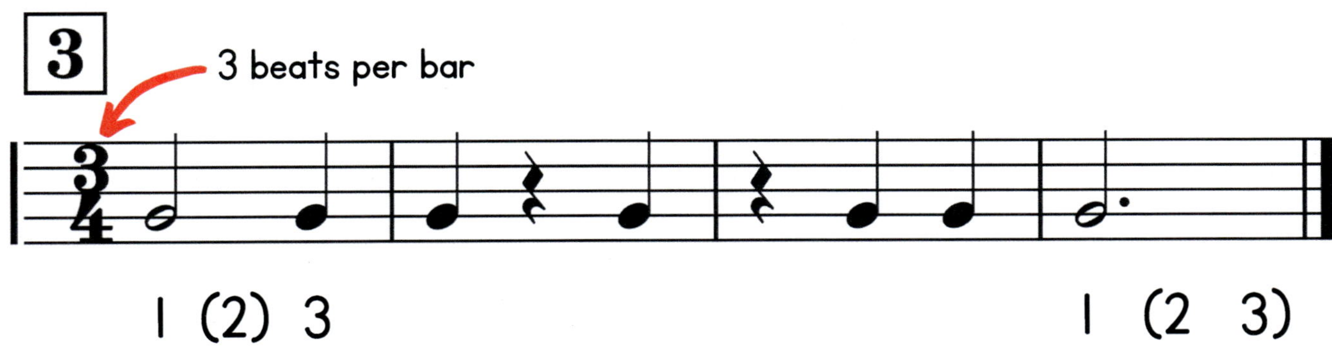

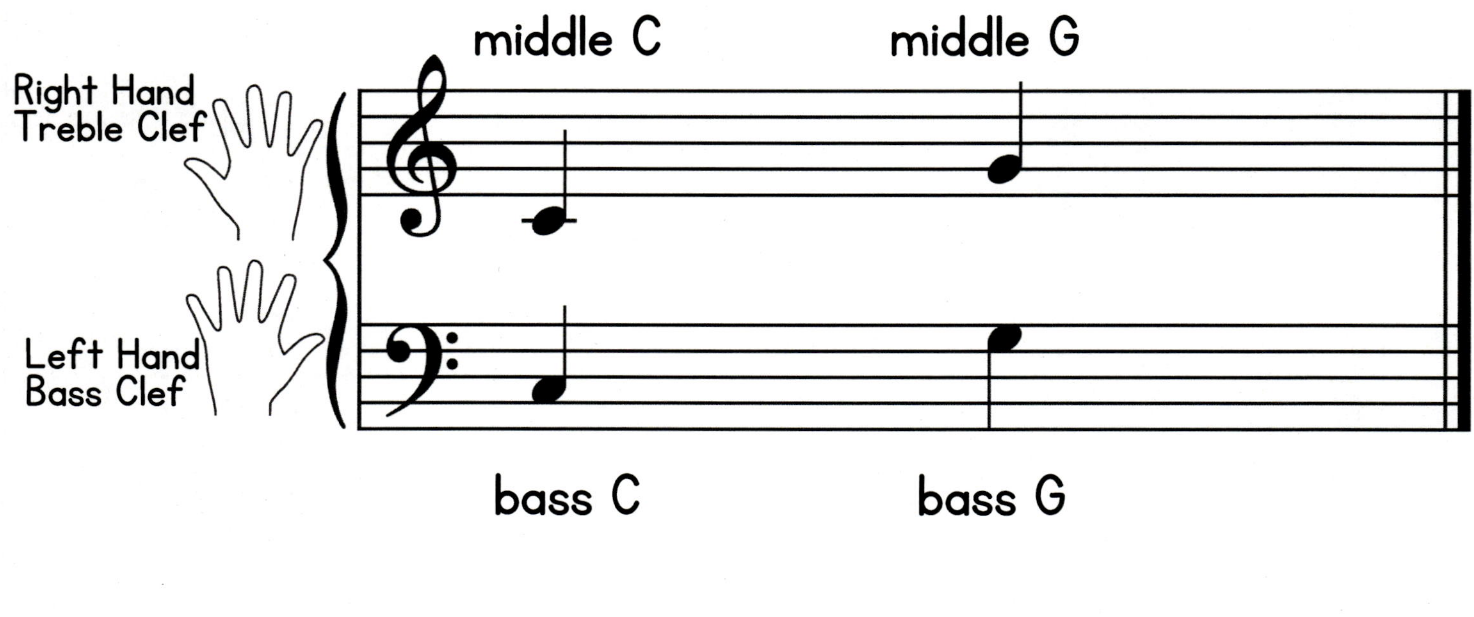
middle C
middle G
Right Hand
Treble Clef
Left Hand
Bass Clef
bass C
bass G

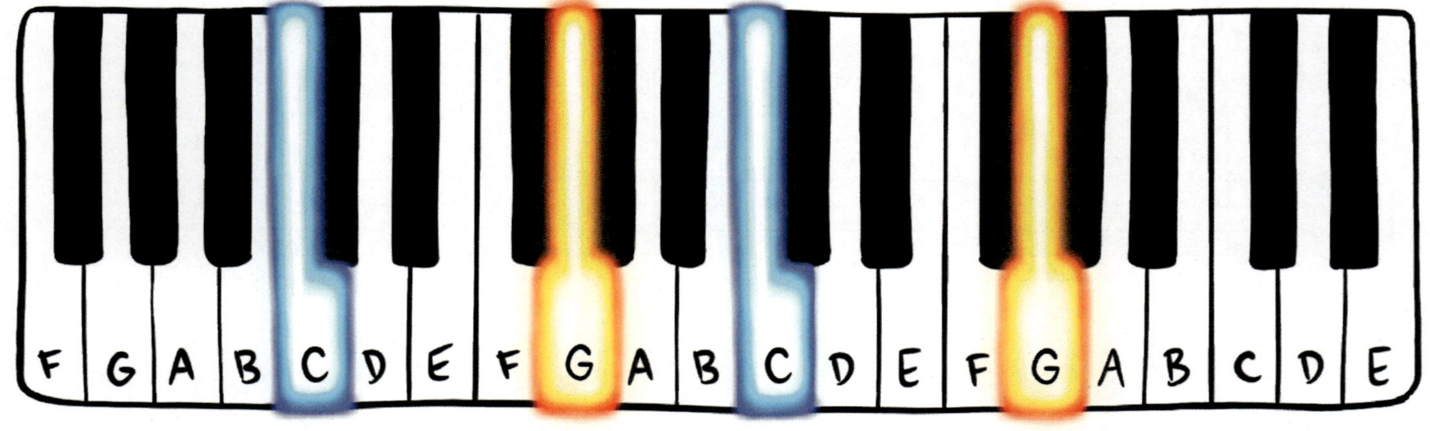
F G A B C D E F G A B C D E F G A B C D E
bass C
bass G
middle C
middle G

Now it's time to play the C-G song!

The C-G Song

Right Hand
Treble Clef

Left Hand
Bass Clef

thumb 1 pinky 5

C G

pinky 5 thumb 1

C G

right

left

together!

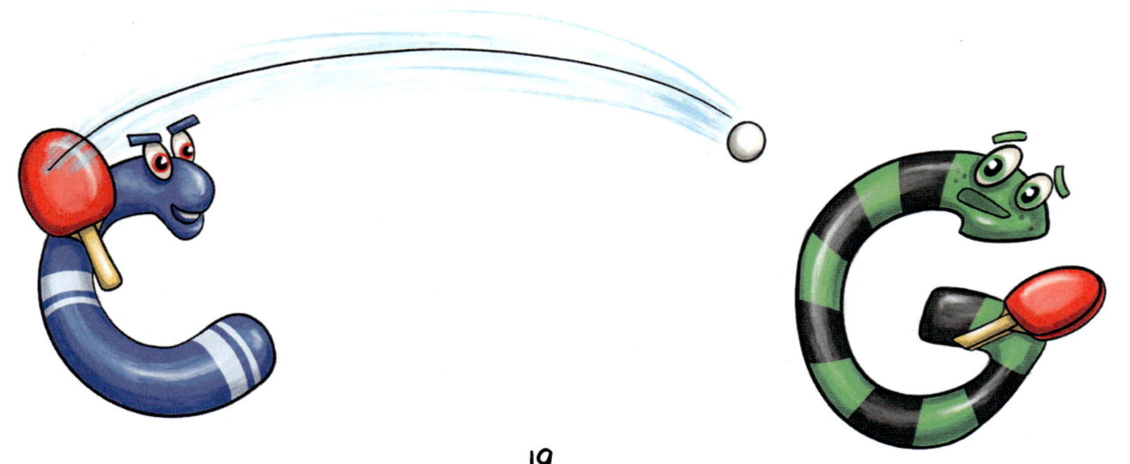

Up, Down, Repeat

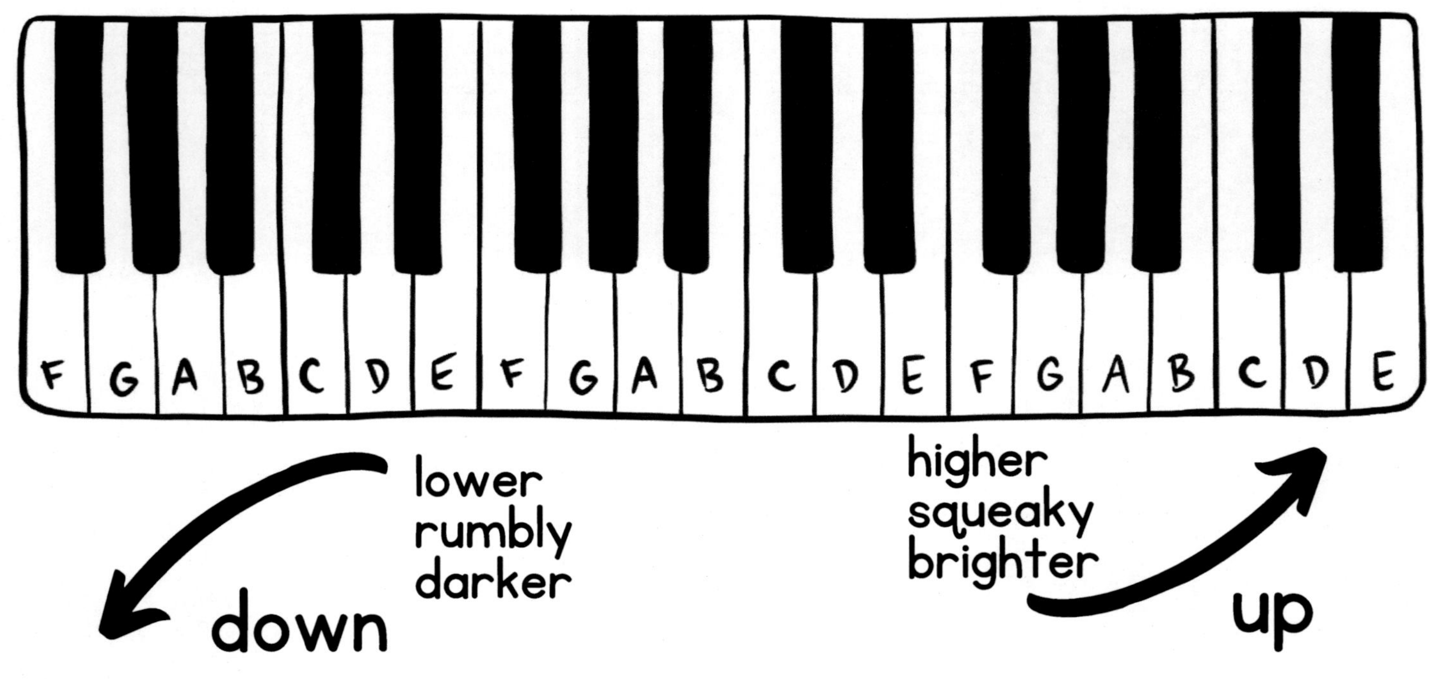

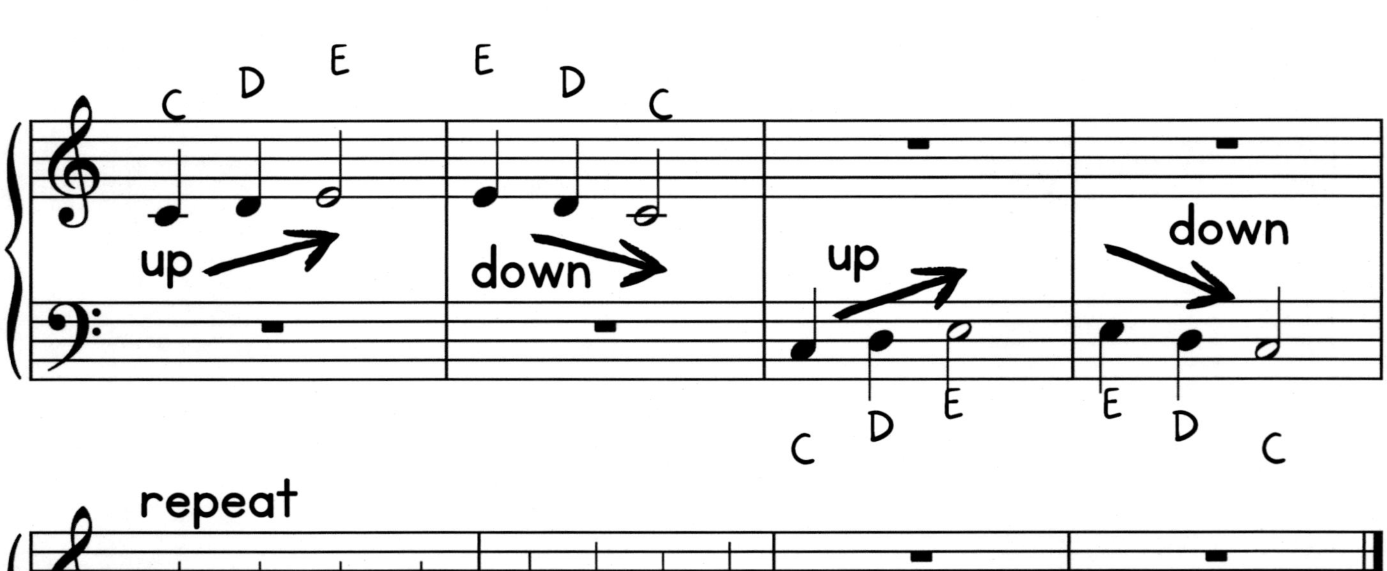

Upstairs Downstairs

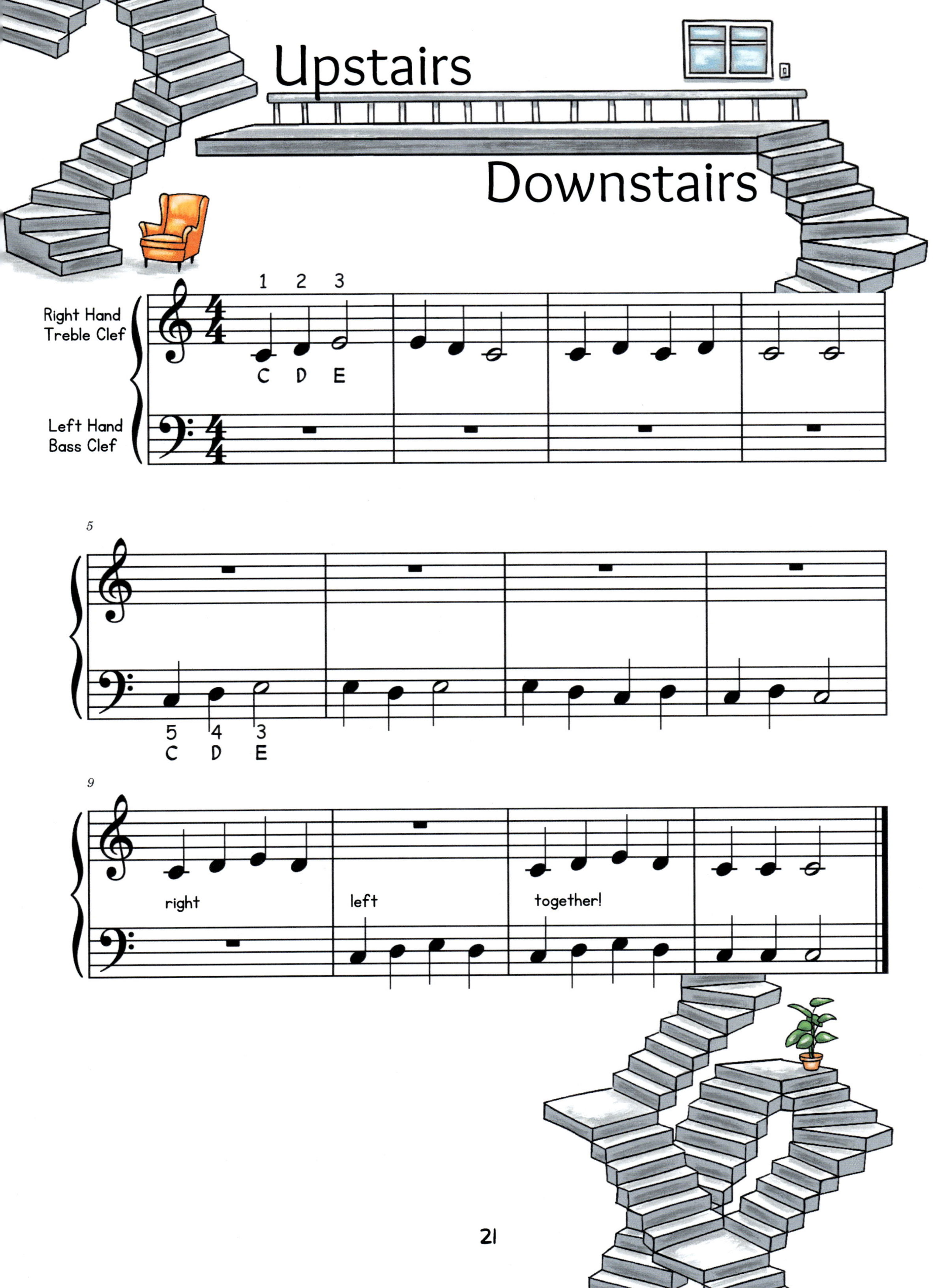

Worksheet: Lines and Spaces

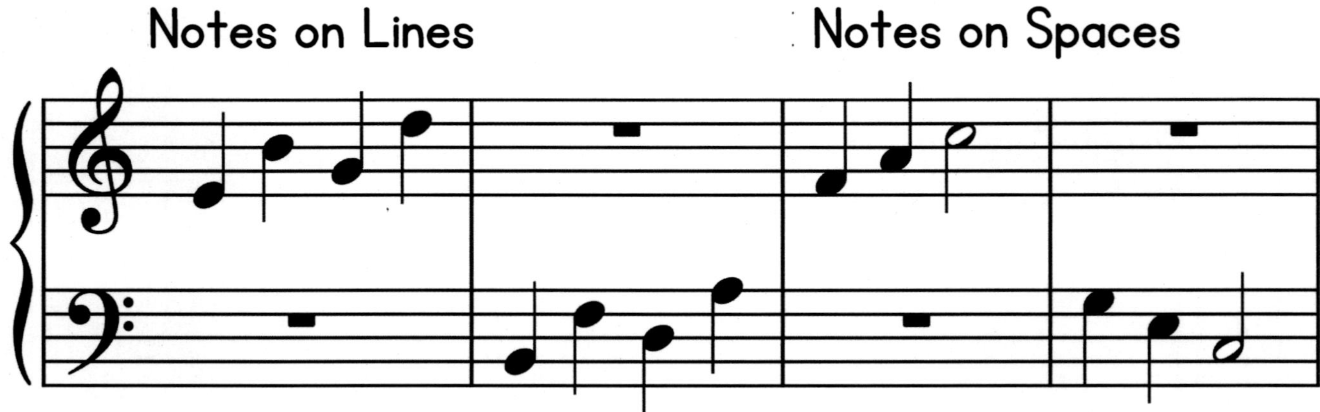

Now practice:

Write L under Line notes and S under Space notes.

Escalators
1 2 3 4
5
C D E F
G
5
5 4 3 2
1
C D E F G
9
left
right
together!

Worksheet: Skips, Steps, and Repeats

Repeats

Now let's practice:

Reading from left to right, write whether the notes are moving in a Skip, a Step, or a Repeat.

Circle the Skips. Write R for Repeat.

SKIPPING STONES

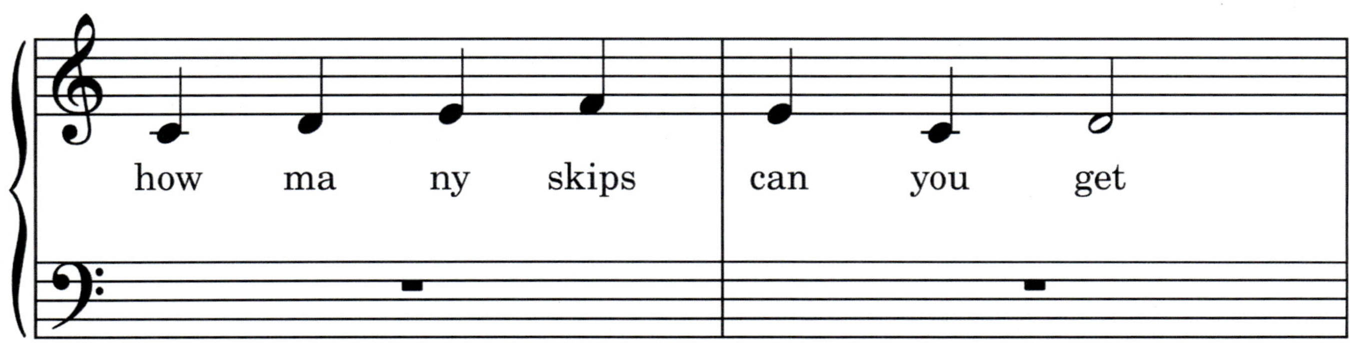

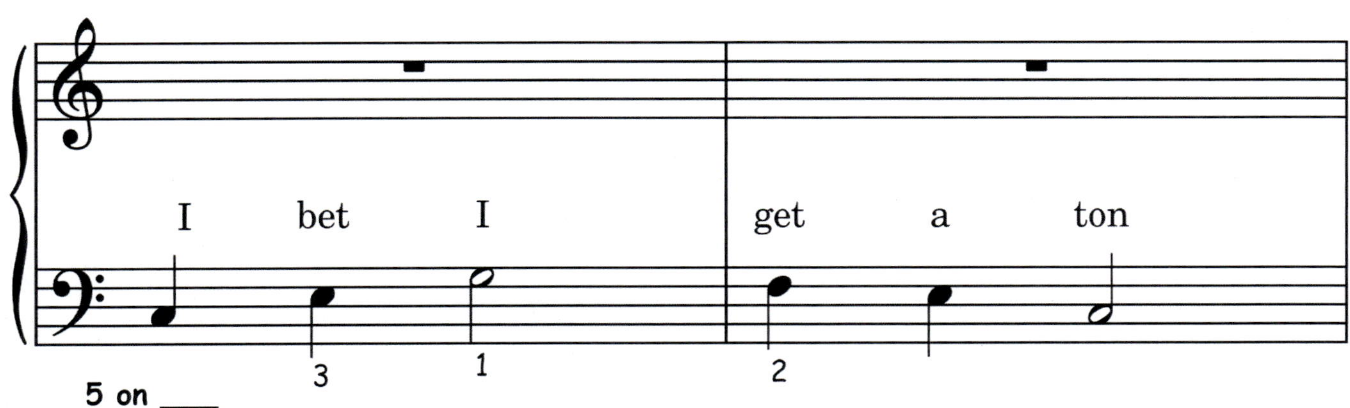

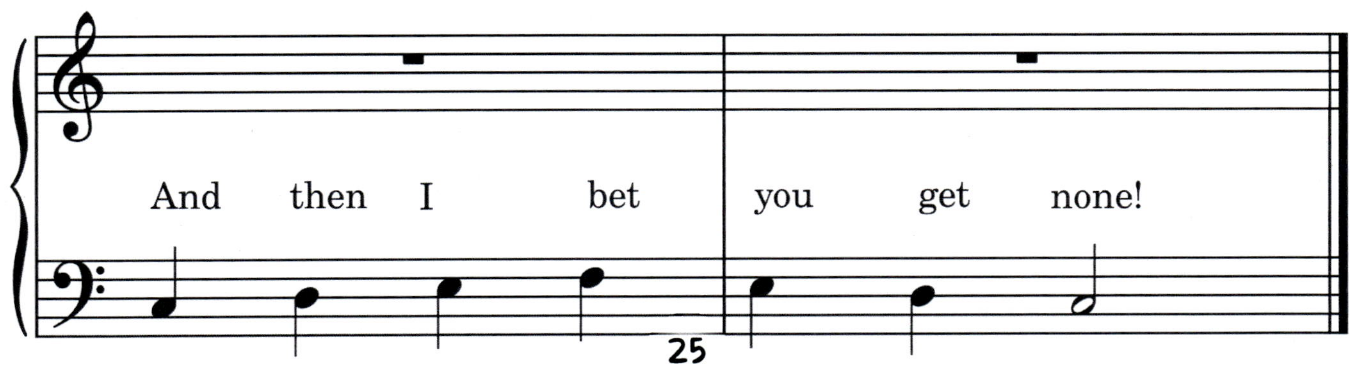

DOG!
1 on ___
This is my dog He's just a pup
5
He's a good boy come say 'what's up!'
This is my dog He is the best
5 on ___
13
He's just a fluff Now let him rest

PIZZA

1 on ___
G
I'd like a piz - za de - li - vered to me

5
F
With ex - tra cheese No an - cho - vies

9
I'd like a piz - za for my din - ner please a
G

5 on ___
13
whole piz - za just for me
PIZZA STORE

Worksheet: The Treble Staff

Let's draw Treble Clefs

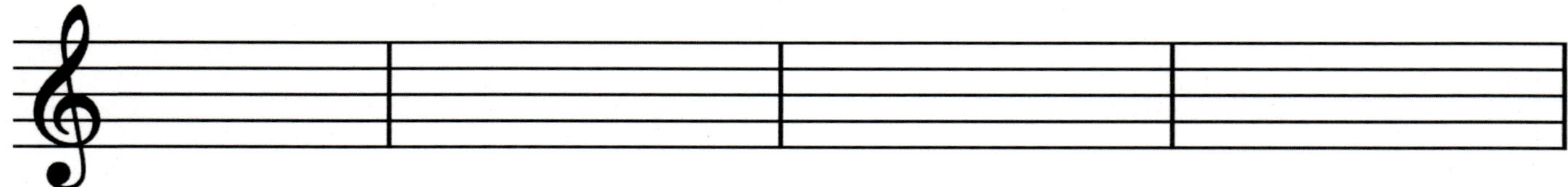

Notes on lines

Name the line notes

Write the name of the note under each note.

Notes on spaces

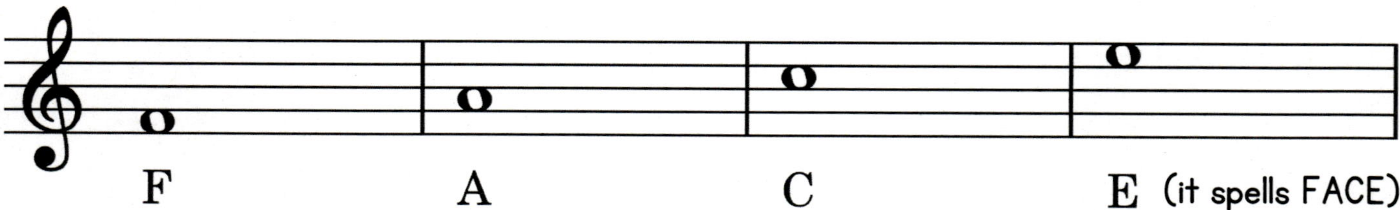

2 Name the space notes

Write the name of the note under each note.

Ledger Lines: Notes above and below the staff

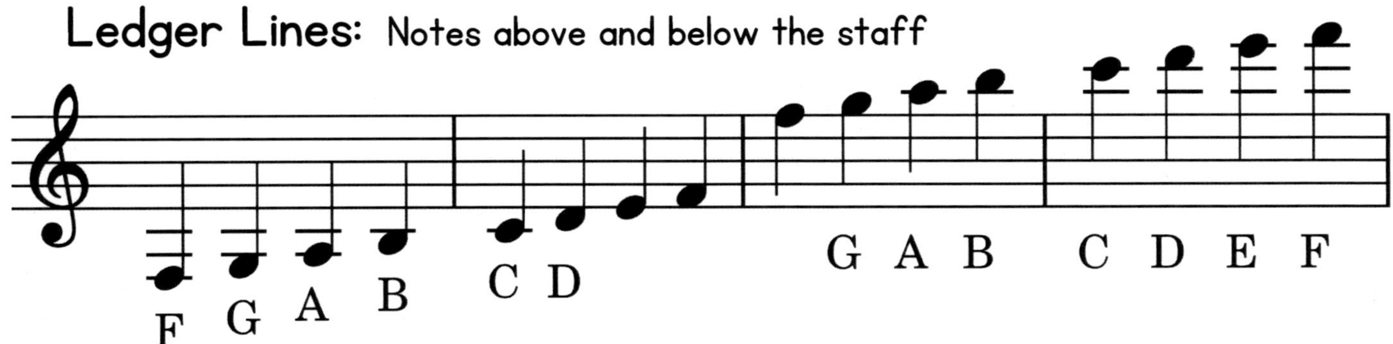

Name the Treble Clef notes

Write the name of the note under each note.

Right Hand Mini Songs

Right Hand the Champion

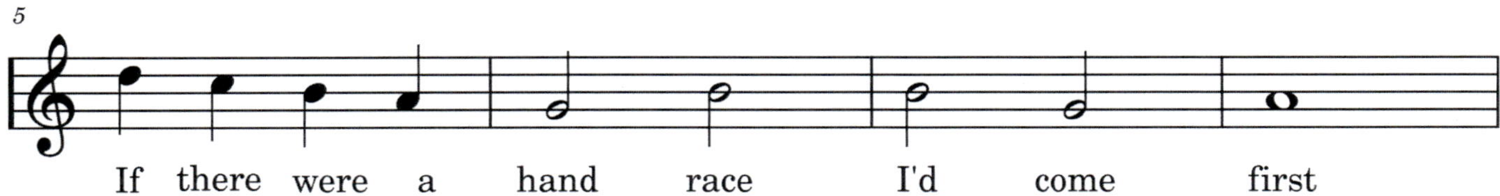

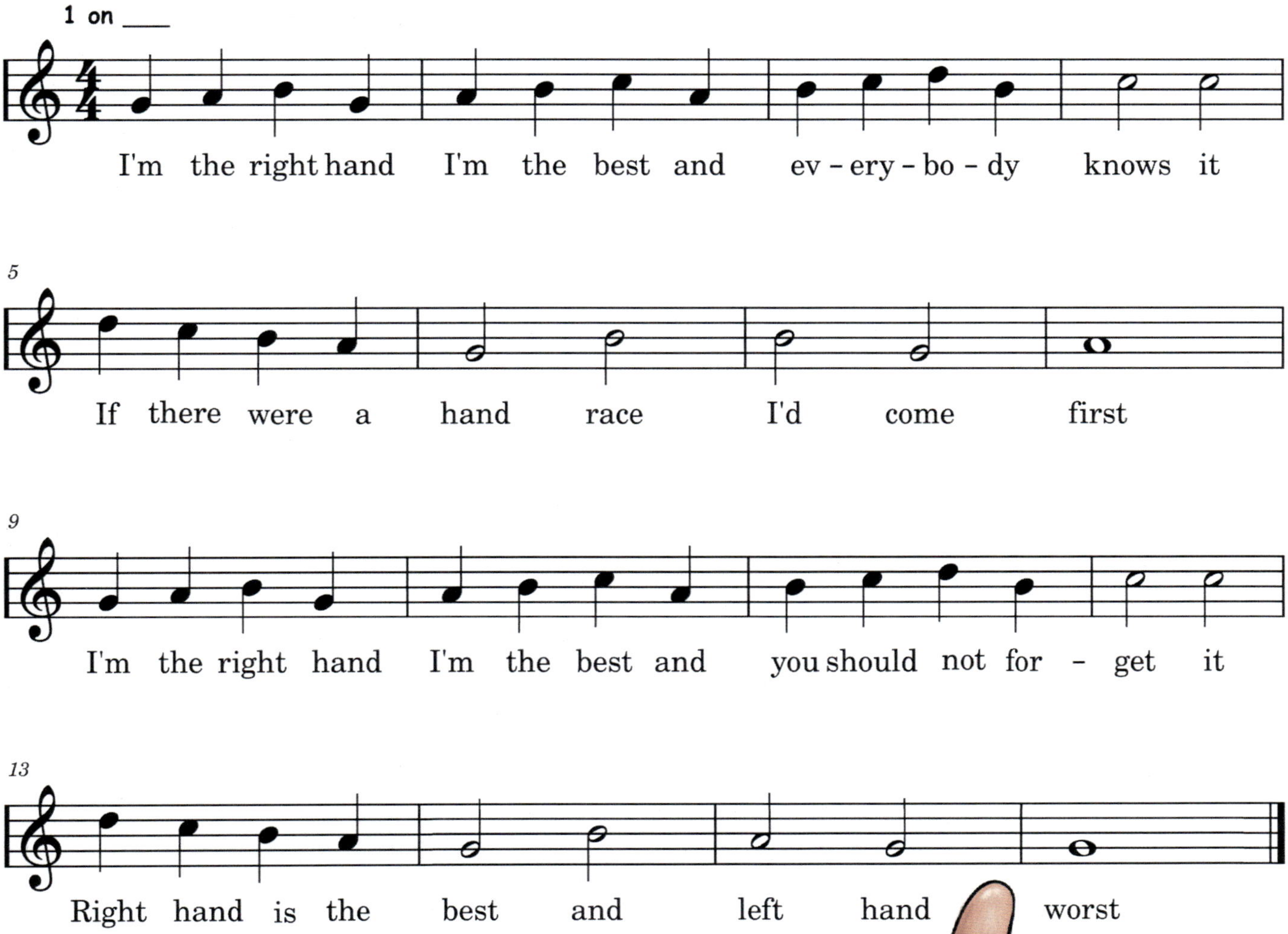

13

Right hand is the best and left hand worst

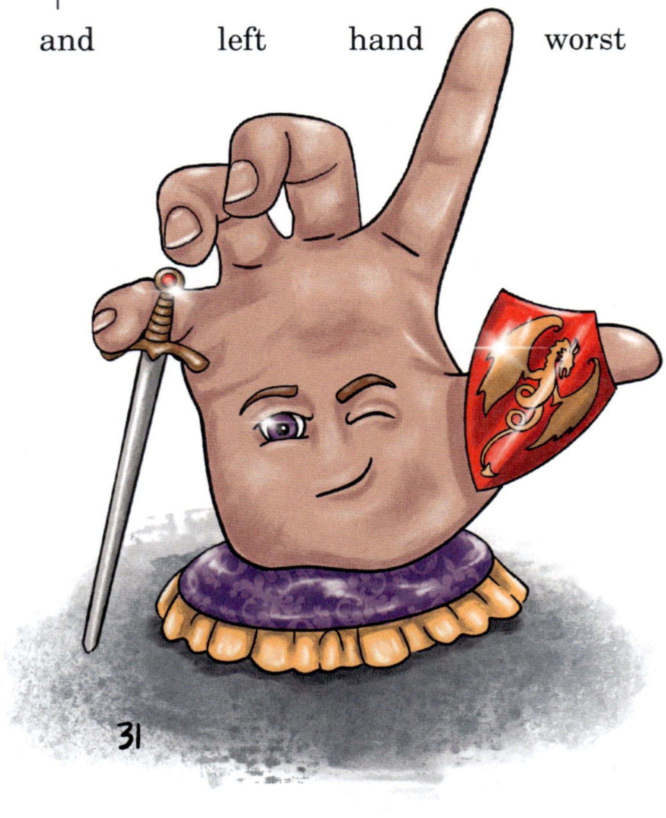

Worksheet: The Bass Staff

Let's draw Bass Clefs

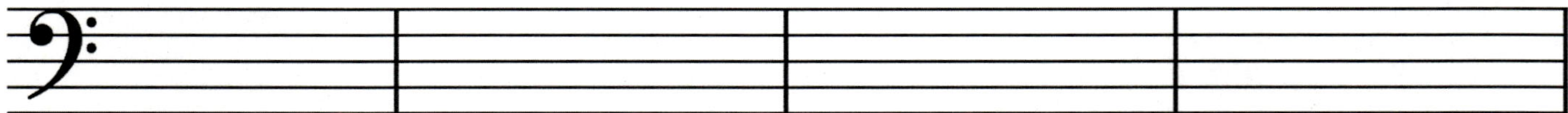

Notes on lines

G	B	D	F	A
Good	Burritos	Don't	Fall	Apart

Name the line notes

Write the name of the note under each note.

Notes on spaces

A	C	E	G
All	Cows	Eat	Grass

2 ## Name the space notes

Write the name of the note under each note.

Ledger Lines: Notes above and below the staff

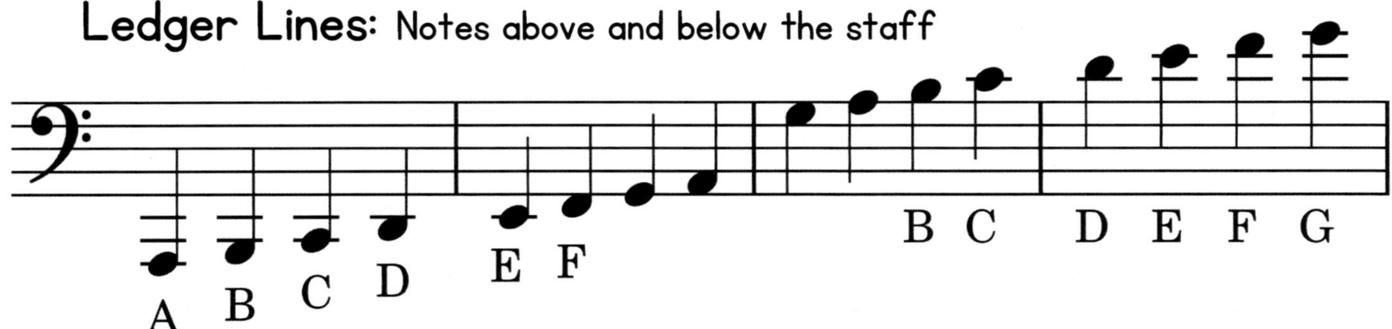

Name the Bass Clef notes

Write the name of the note under each note.

34

Left Hand Mini Songs

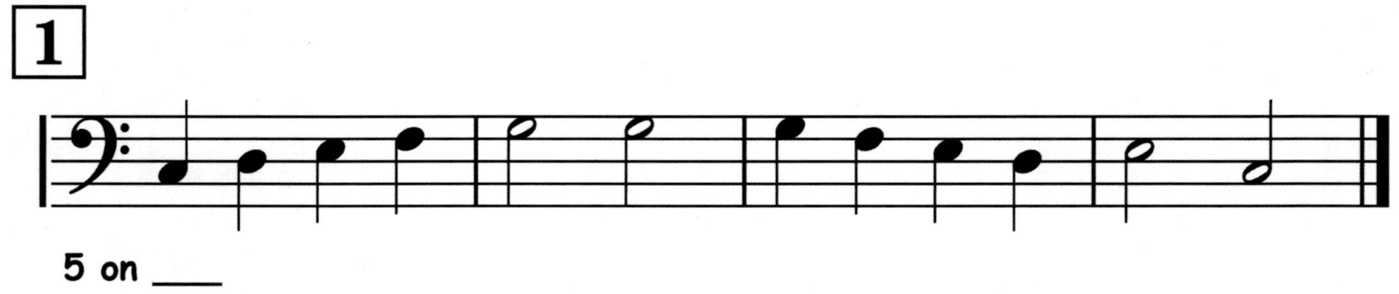

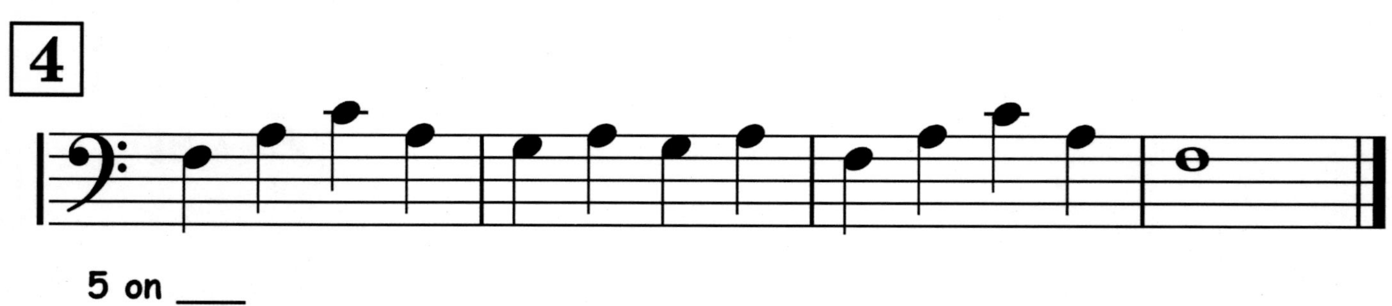

Left Hand Sad

1 on ___

5
D

Why does right hand al - ways get the

Notes on the Piano

Hand Warm-ups

5 Note Warm-up

Play this Hands Together

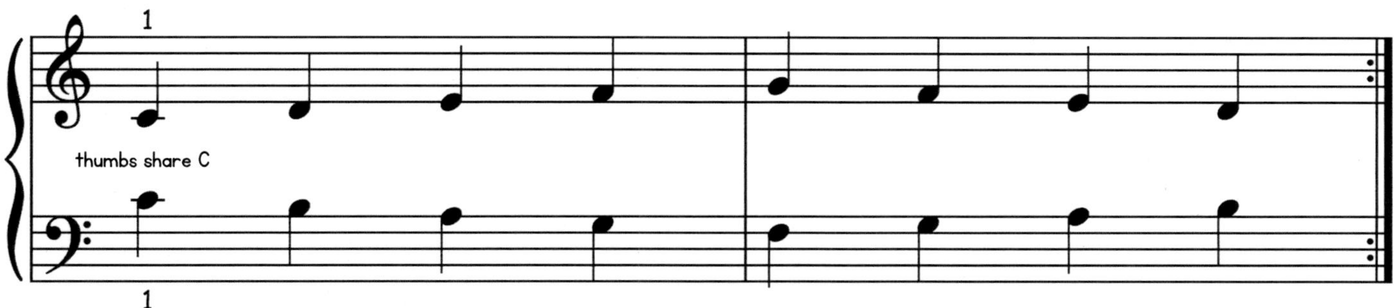

C Scale

Play this Hands Separately

When you want to, try playing it Hands Together!

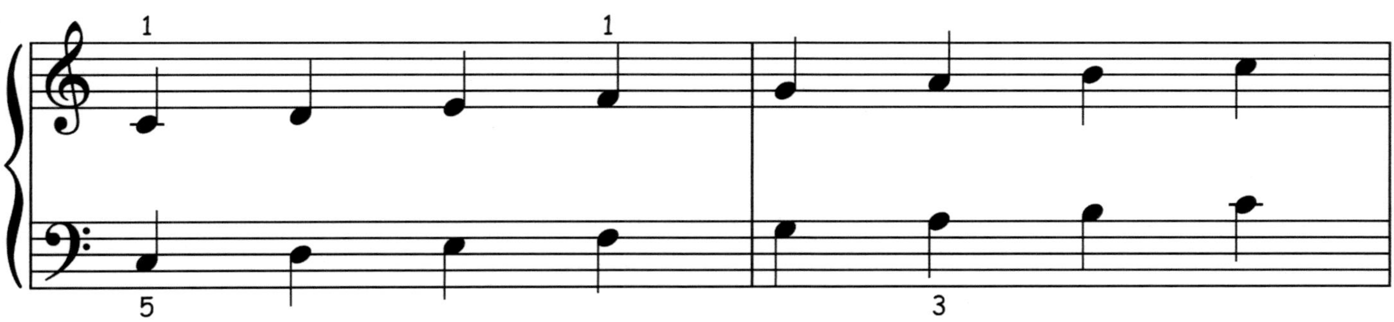

Fish

1 on ___

I am just a lit - tle fish I have on - ly just one wish Feeeeeed Meeeeee

2 on ___

Lots of fish - y food

CAR GO ZOOM ZOOM FAST

MUSIC IS AWESOME

5 on ___

13

Mu - sic is the best sub-ject in school

KOALA

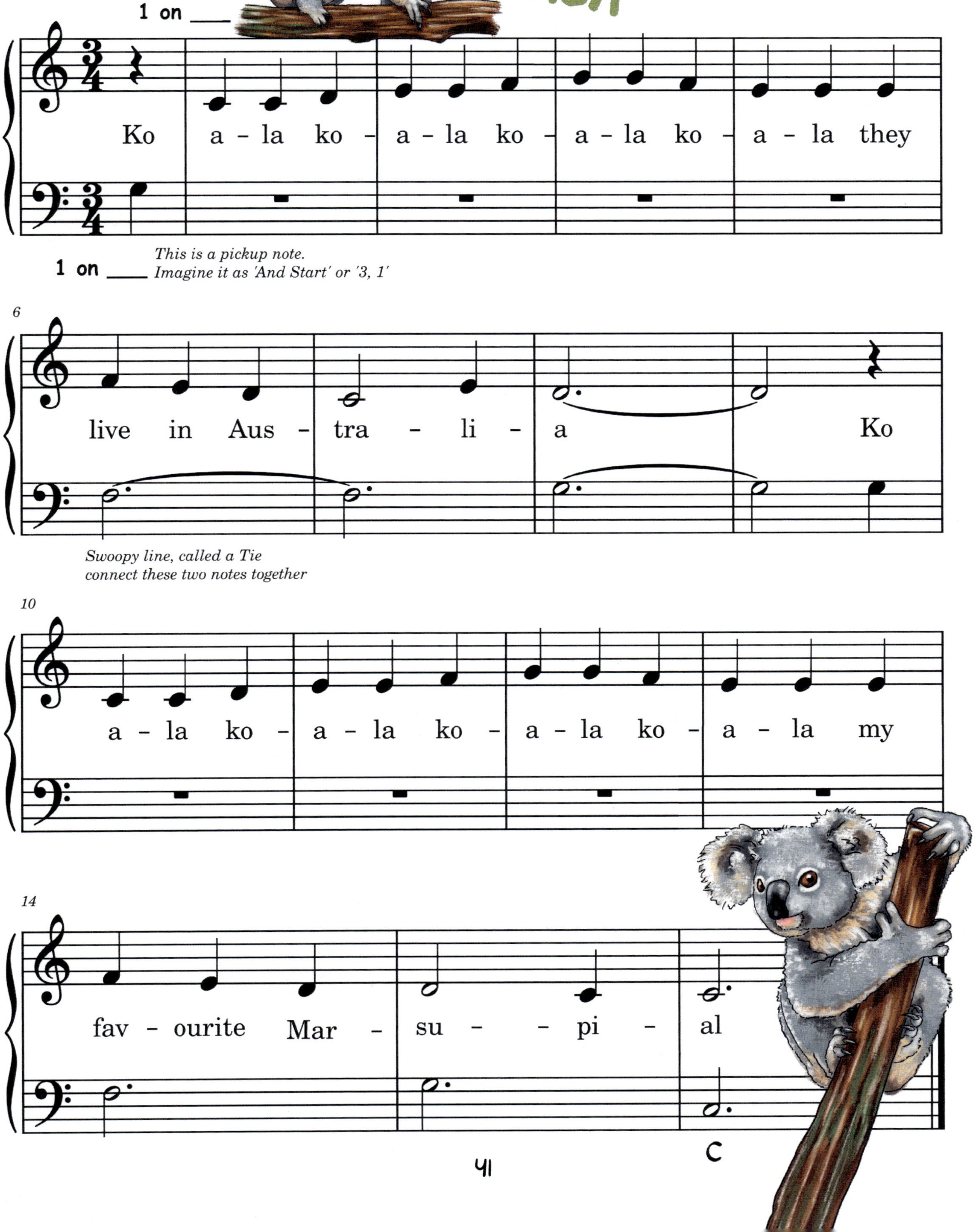

1 on ___ *This is a pickup note.*
Imagine it as 'And Start' or '3, 1'

Swoopy line, called a Tie
connect these two notes together

10

a - la ko - a - la ko - a - la ko - a - la my

14

fav - ourite Mar - su - - pi - al

C

LEMONADE
LEMONADE PROFITS
PROFITS
DATE
1 on ___
D
Notes stacked on top of each other: play these at the same time.
"Would you like a le - mon - ade?"
1
3
5 on ___
5
"Yes I rea - lly would!"
9
D
"That will be one thou-sand dol-lars."
C
"Why
13
sir that is abs - urd!"

Accidentals

♯ = Sharp ♭ = Flat

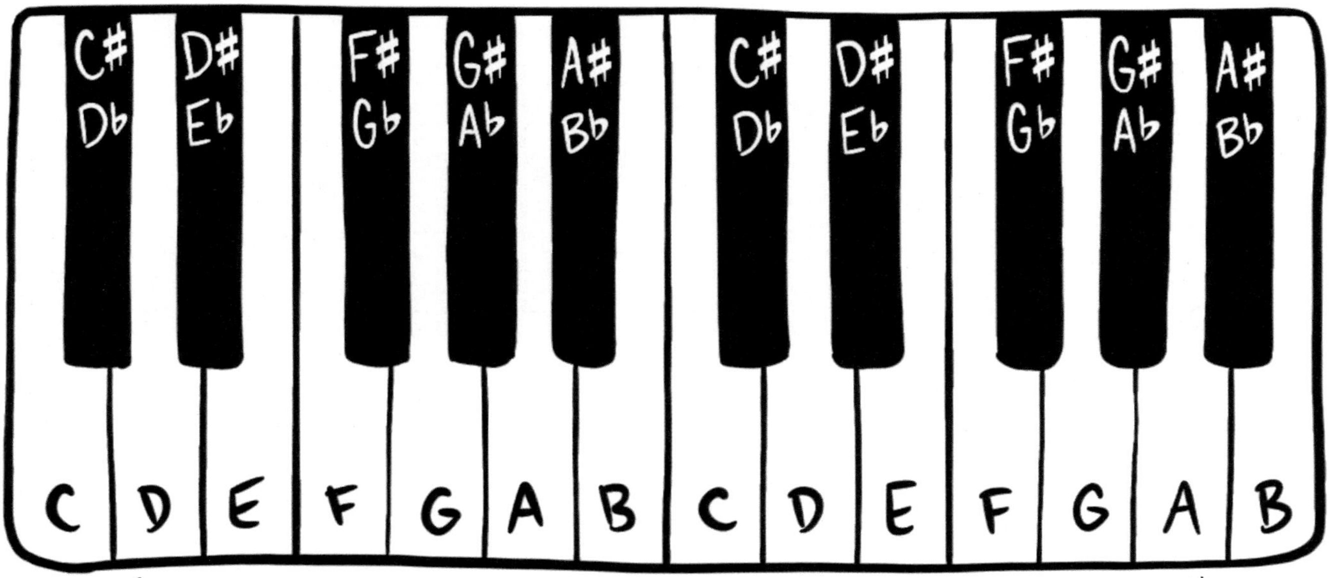

C♯ D♯ F♯ G♯ A♯ C♯ D♯ F♯ G♯ A♯
D♭ E♭ G♭ A♭ B♭ D♭ E♭ G♭ A♭ B♭

C D E F G A B C D E F G A B

← ♭ Flat is to the left
= lower

Sharp is to the right ♯ →
= higher

♮ = Natural

If a note gets flattened or sharpened in a bar, it stays that way until the end of the bar, or until it gets a natural symbol on it (which makes it a regular "natural" note again).

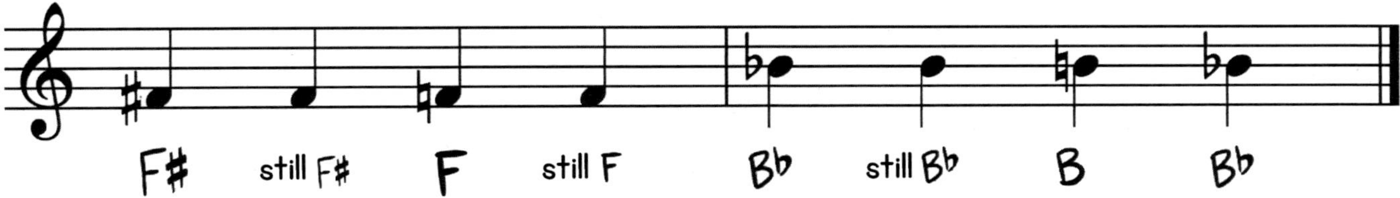

SUNNY DAY BIKE RIDE
1 on ___
3
4
5
A
D
5
9
Cross your 2nd finger
Over your thumb
13
2
1

Jungle Party
1 on ___
Welc-ome to our jung-le part-y
High D (Octave!)
Low D
5
We've got lots of things to do
Reach your thumb for the C
Then return it for the D
9
1 2 1
We can swing on vines all even-ing
13
1 2 1
Bet - ter than your loc - al zoo
45

MARTIAN FRIENDS

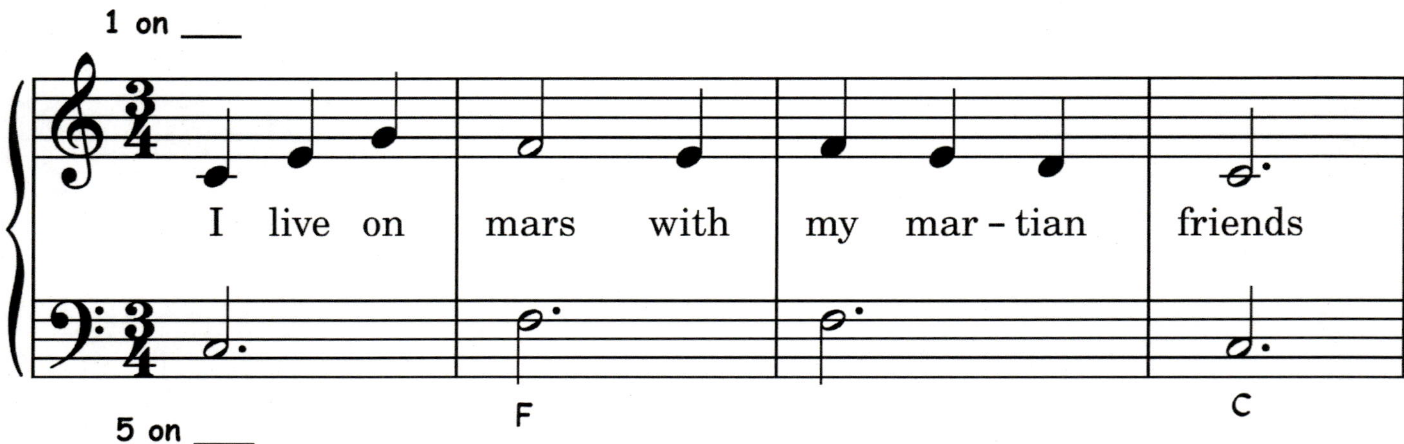

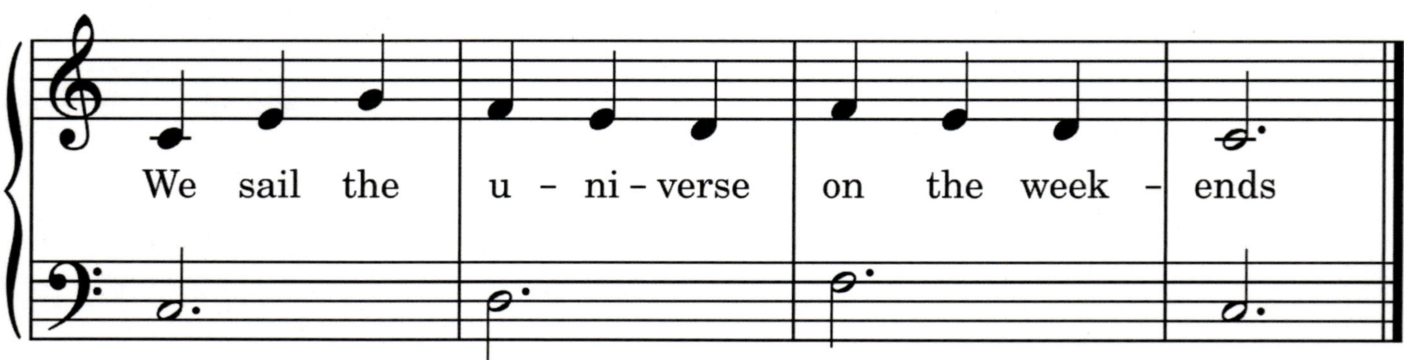

Hot Air Balloon

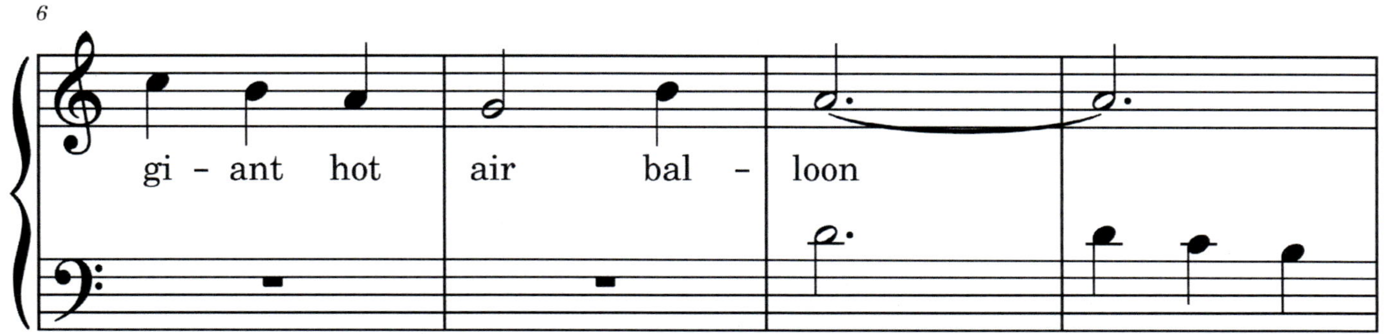

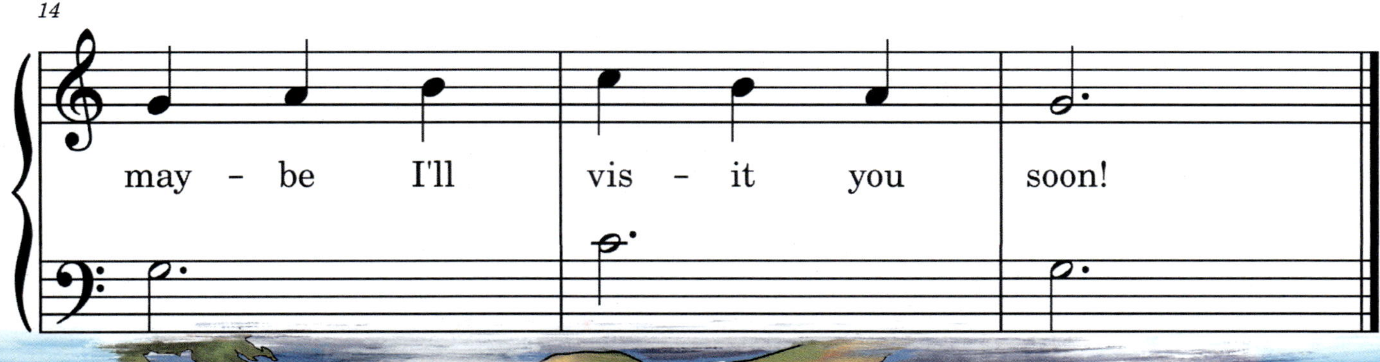

Chords

Let's look at these two kinds of chords:

Today, let's say: C chord starts on C,
D chord starts on D, and so on...

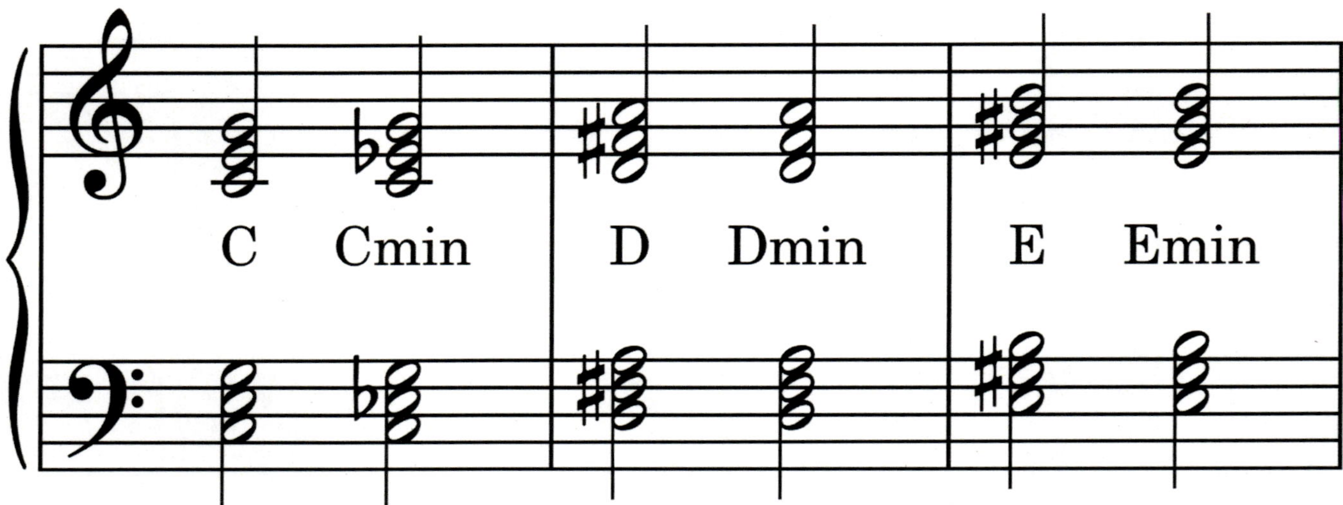

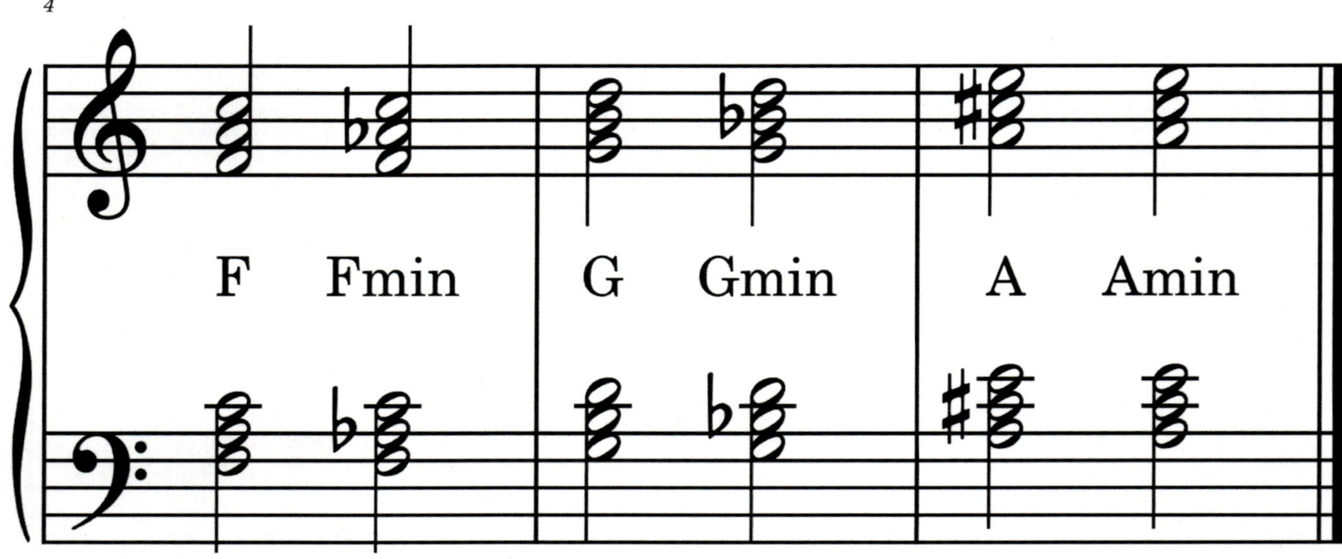

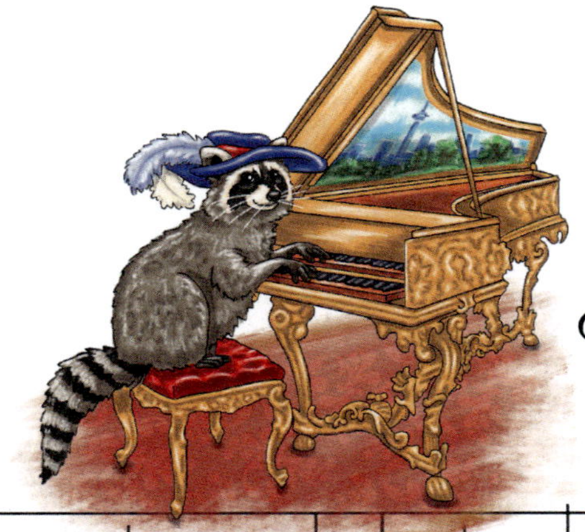

Fancy Little Song

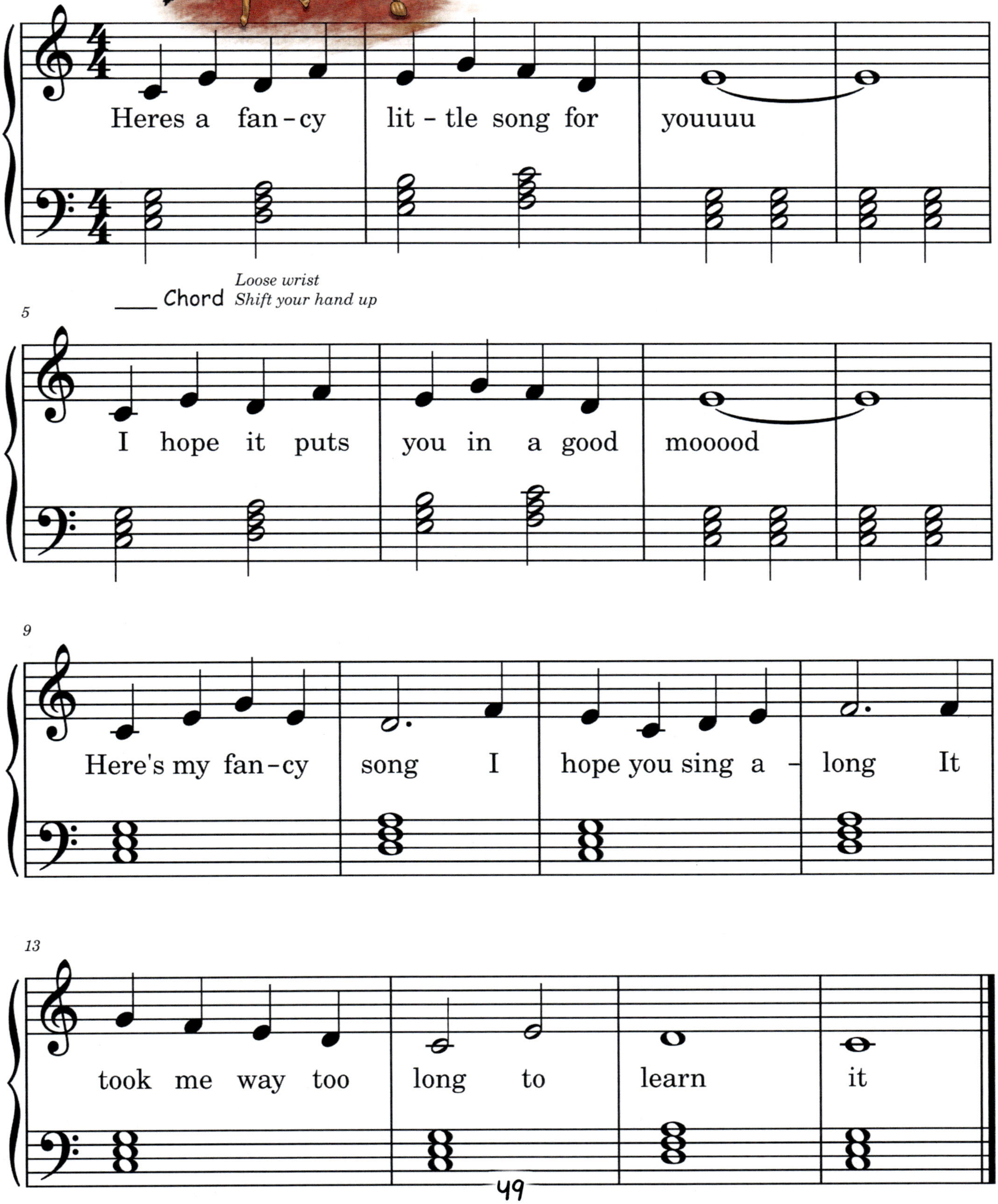

Heres a fan-cy lit-tle song for youuuu

___ Chord *Loose wrist* *Shift your hand up*

5

I hope it puts you in a good mooood

9

Here's my fan-cy song I hope you sing a-long It

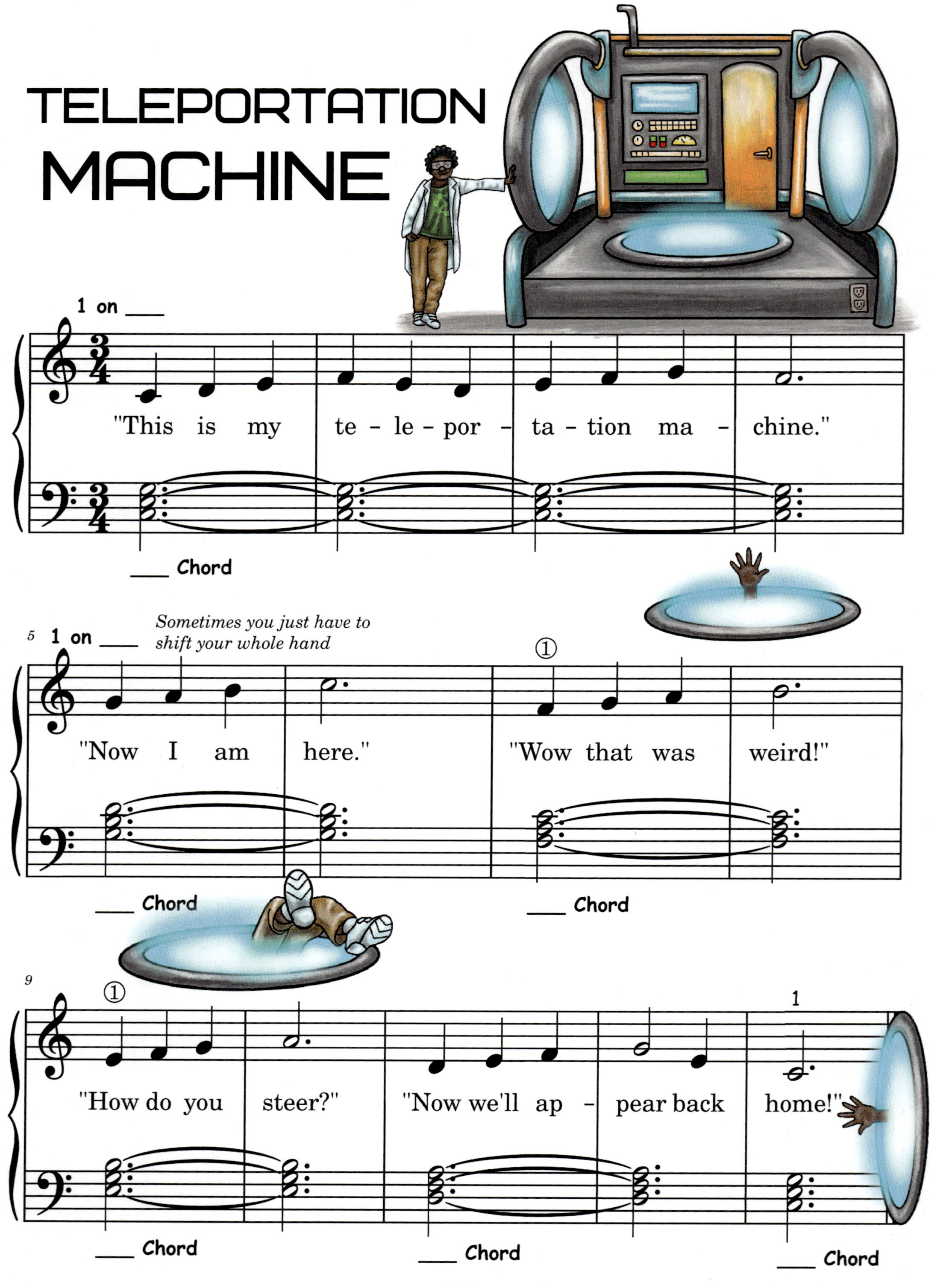
TELEPORTATION MACHINE
1 on ___
"This is my te - le - por - ta - tion ma - chine."
___ Chord
5
1 on ___
Sometimes you just have to shift your whole hand
①
"Now I am here."
"Wow that was weird!"
___ Chord
___ Chord
9
①
1
"How do you steer?"
"Now we'll ap - pear back home!"
___ Chord
___ Chord
___ Chord

GIANT CAT WITH LASER BEAMS
1 on ___
Watch out for the gi-ant cat with la - ser beams It
___ Chord
___ Chord
___ Chord
5
may look fluf - fy but it will des - troy you
5 on ___
9
(higher D)
Meow Meow Meow! Meow Meow Meow!
(super low D)
13
Ev - il kit - ty Ev - il Kit - ty Ev - il kit - ty cat!

TRAMPOLINE

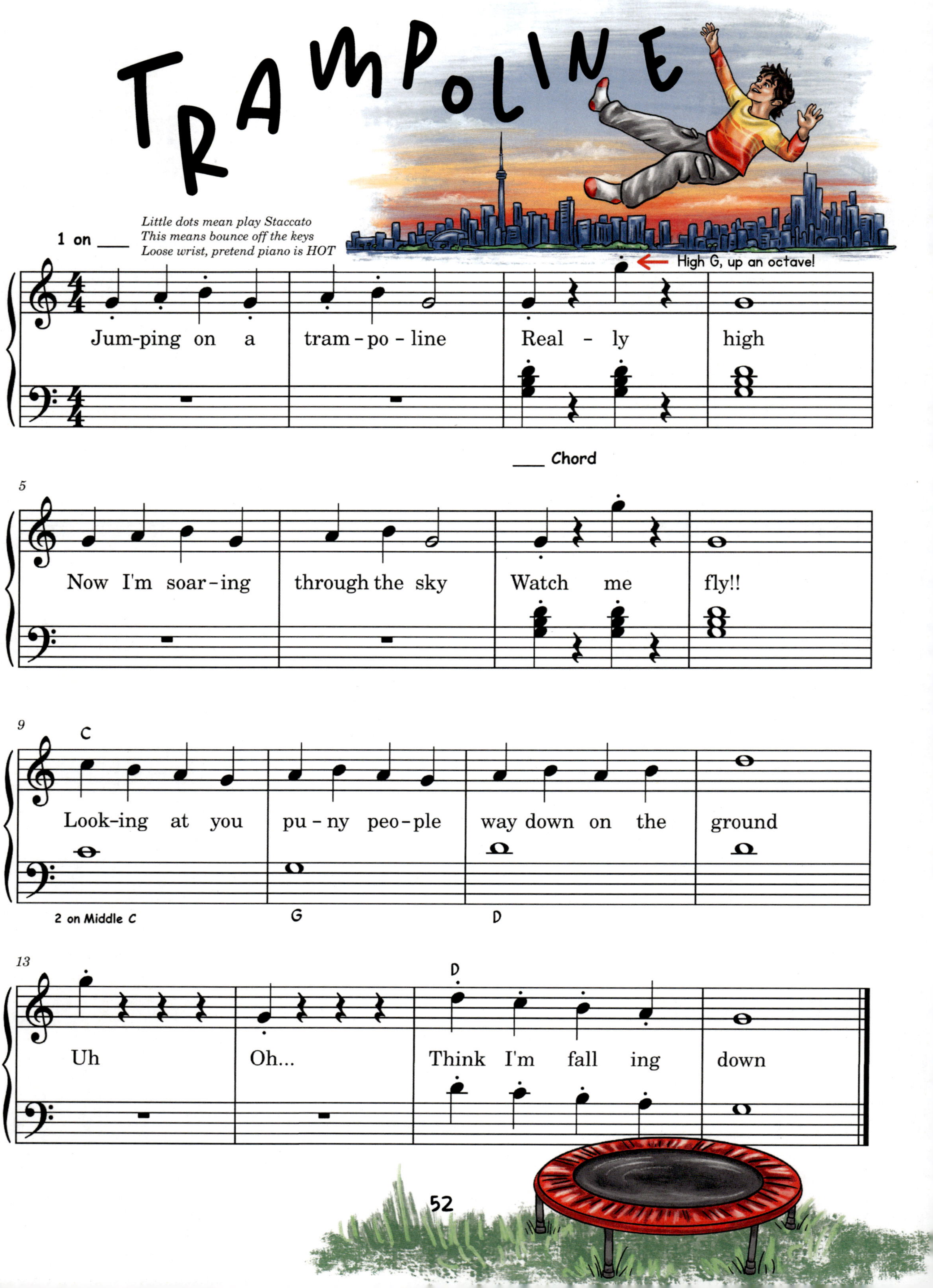

Little dots mean play Staccato
This means bounce off the keys
Loose wrist, pretend piano is HOT

1 on ___

High G, up an octave!

Jum-ping on a tram-po-line Real - ly high

___ Chord

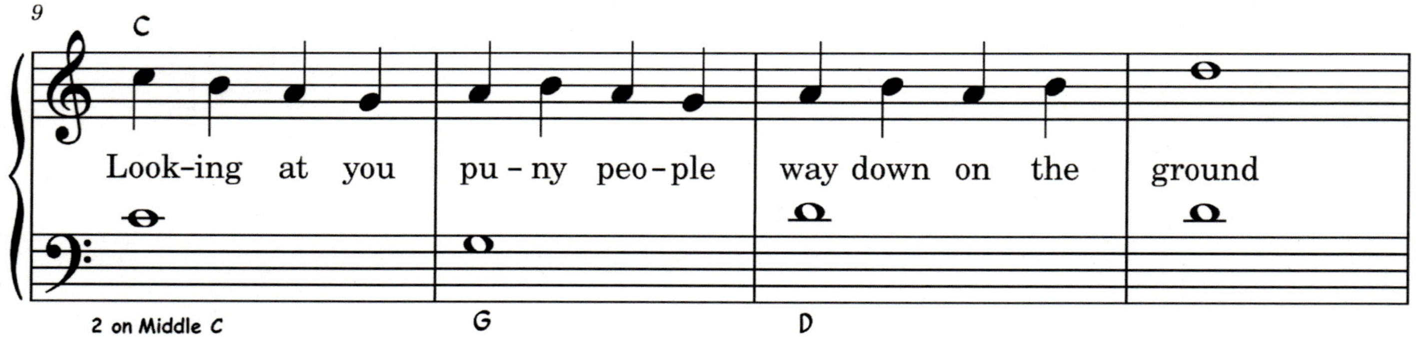

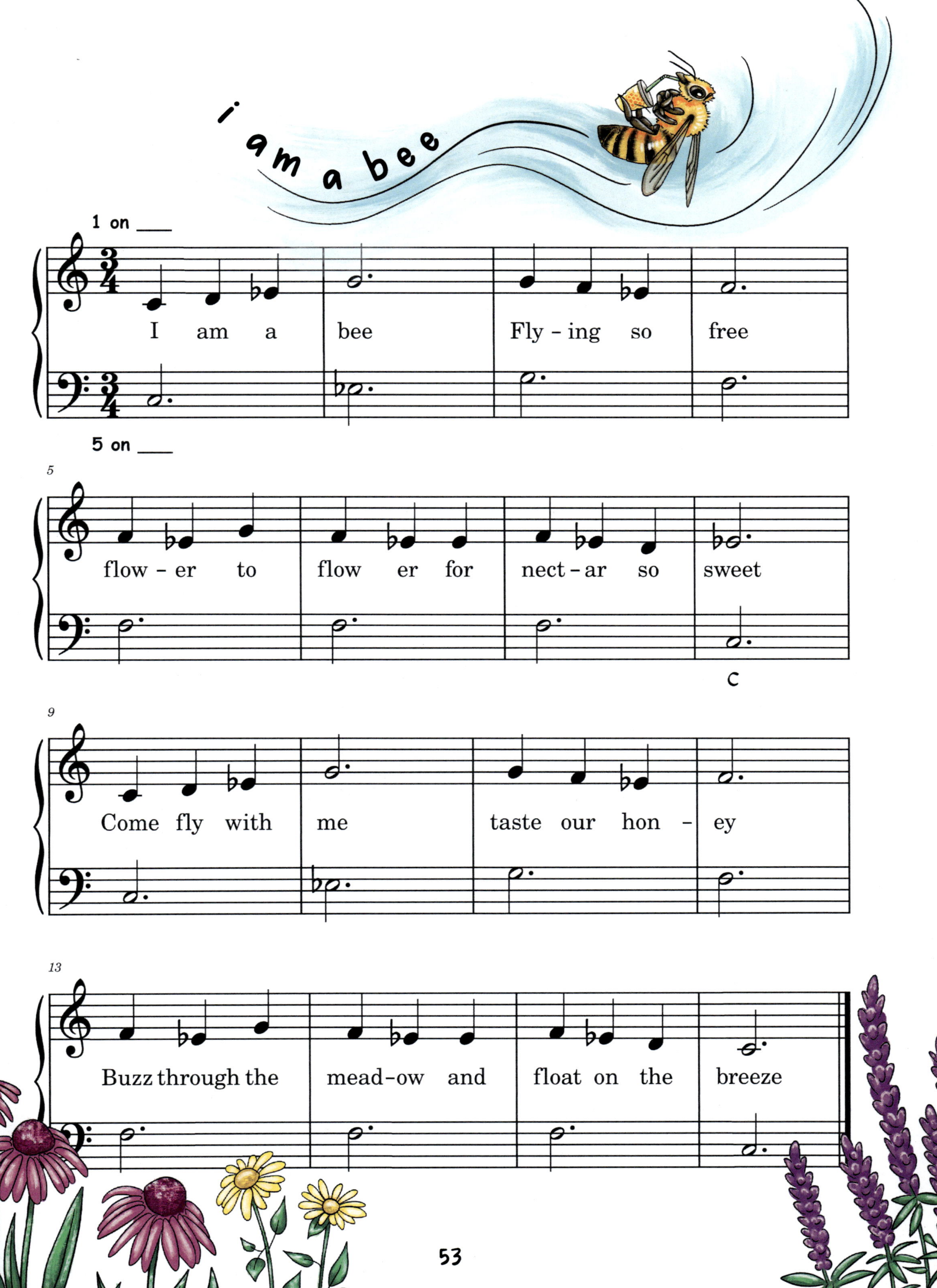
i am a bee
1 on ___
I am a bee
Fly - ing so free
5 on ___
flow - er to flow er for nect - ar so sweet
C
Come fly with me
taste our hon - ey
Buzz through the mead-ow and float on the breeze

OGRE
1 on ___
Eyes and nose and Clun-ky toes I'm stomp-ing big and green I've
1 on ___
5
been an og - re since Oc - to - ber this past hal - lo - ween I
A
E
9
Made a wish and now I'm this but I can't seem to change
13
Back in - to the kid I knew it just can't be ar - ranged
54

Pirate Ship
1 on ___
Welc-ome to my pi-rate ship
Thumb cross under
5 on ___
We sail the seas of the world
Reset pinky on A
Out for a thrill? Then come sail at will un-
A
less you get sea - sick and hurl!

Climbing a tree
1 on ___
Cross your thumb under your 3rd finger
1 2
Climb-ing a tree til I reach the top
F
G
5 on ___
5
Reach
1
Cross over
2
Look-ing straight down Hope I don't drop
9
1
1
1
Climb-ing a tree till I'm king of the land From
13
here you look like an ant!

The Adventure's Just Begun

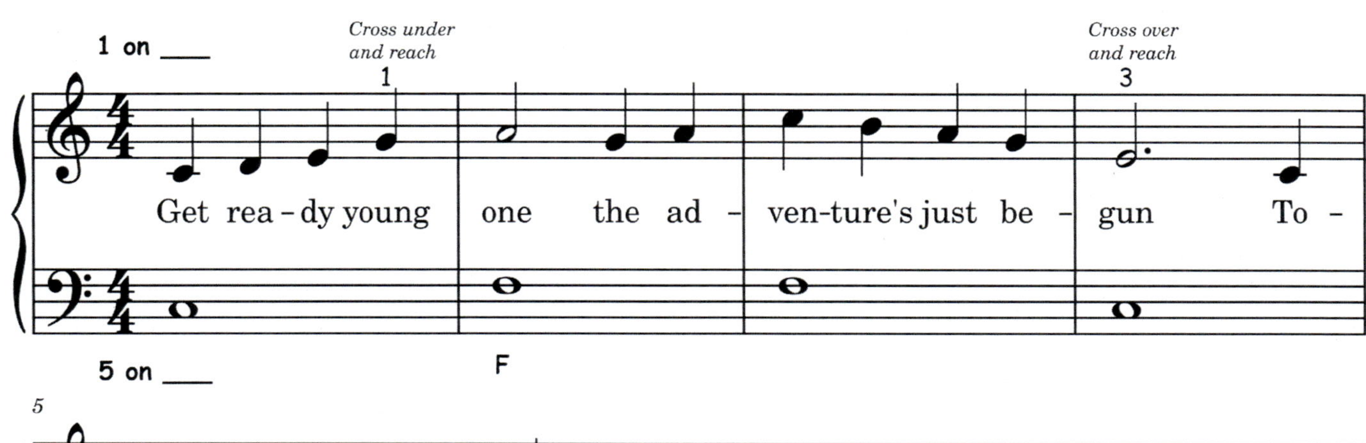

Eighth Notes

eighth notes	1 +	2 +	3 +	4 +
quarter notes	1	2	3	4
half notes	1	2	3	4
whole note	1	2	3	4

Eighth Note Practice

Clap these and count out loud!

HOMEWORK GO
ROBOT FRIEND
Double dots on darker bar line means repeat this line.
G
5 on ___ G
Here's my clan - ky ro - bot friend
I think he is cool
He does all my home-work now
Now I don't need school!

POTATO

5 on ___
Po - ta - to
Po - ta - to
Ea - ten so ma-ny
ways
5 on ___
You are my
fav-ourite food
I could eat you ev - ery
day

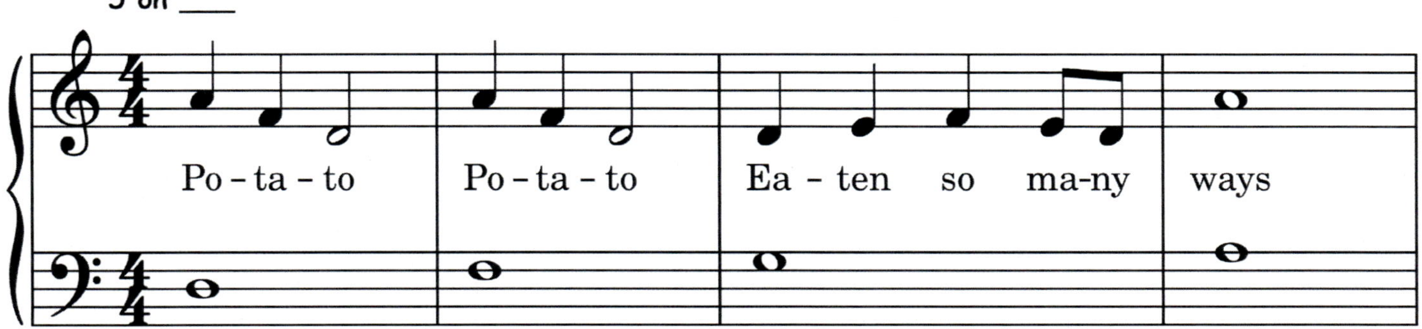

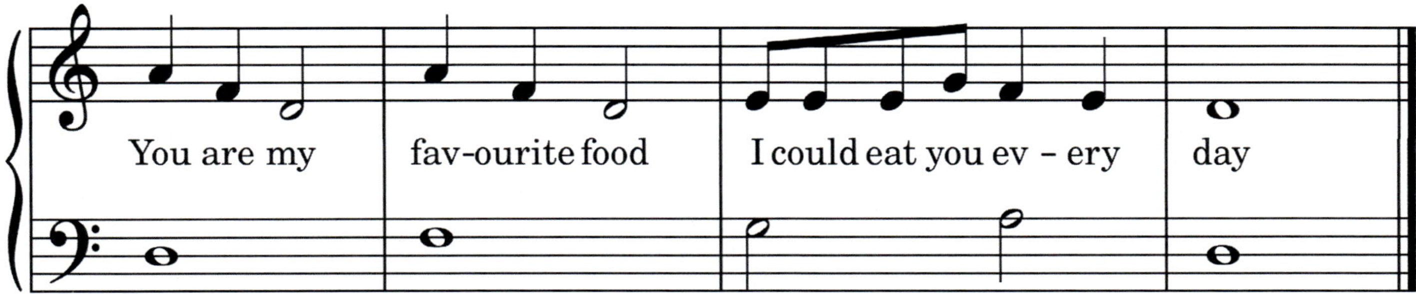

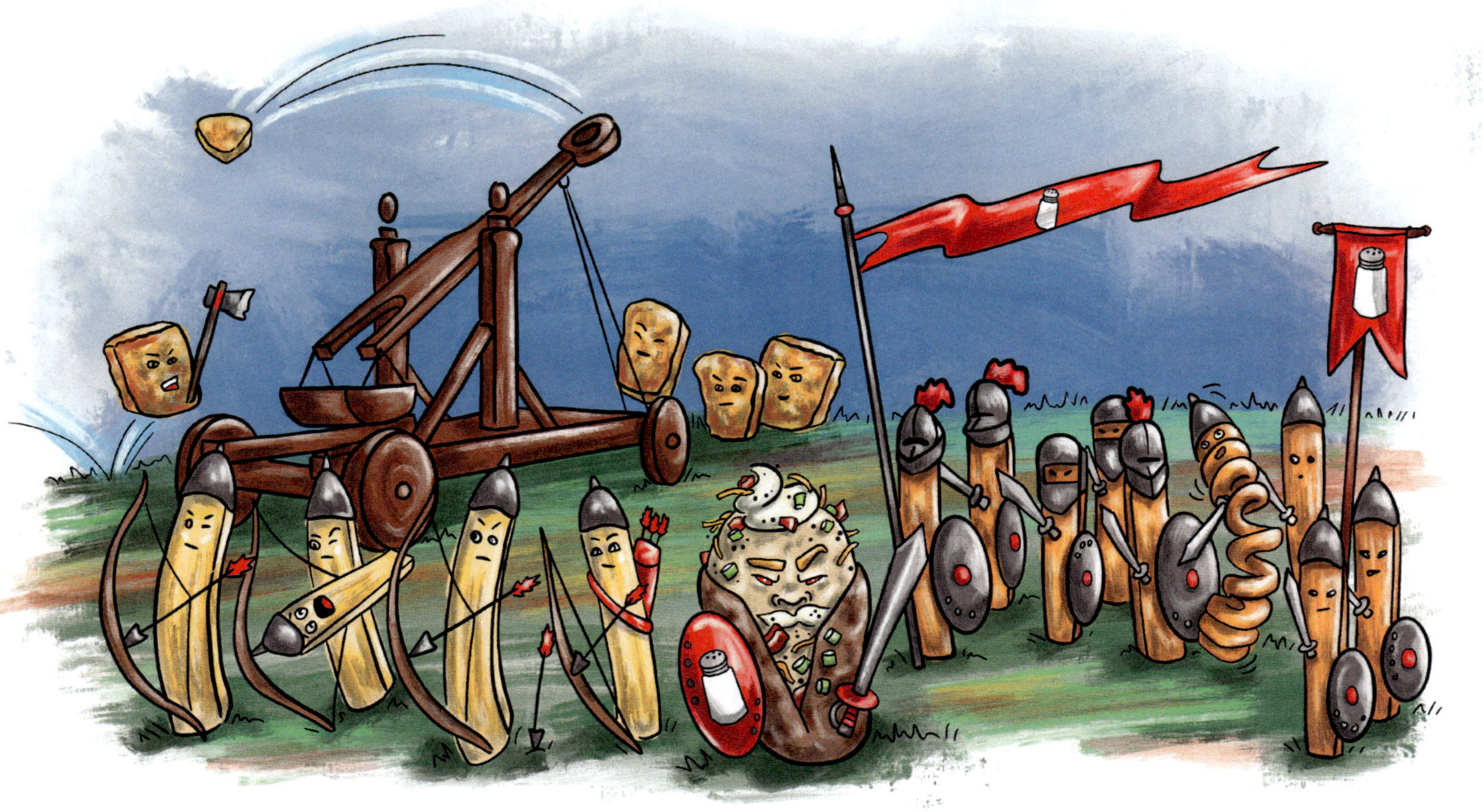

Doug the Slug

1 on ___

1 on ___

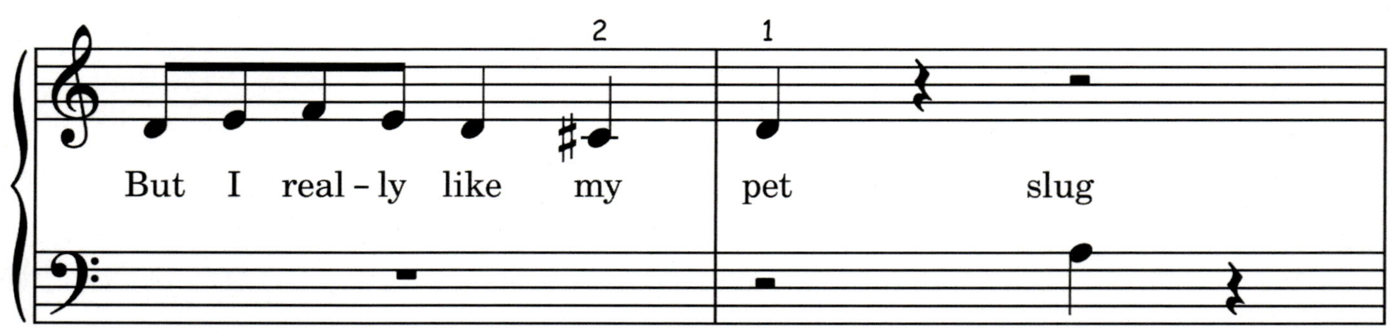

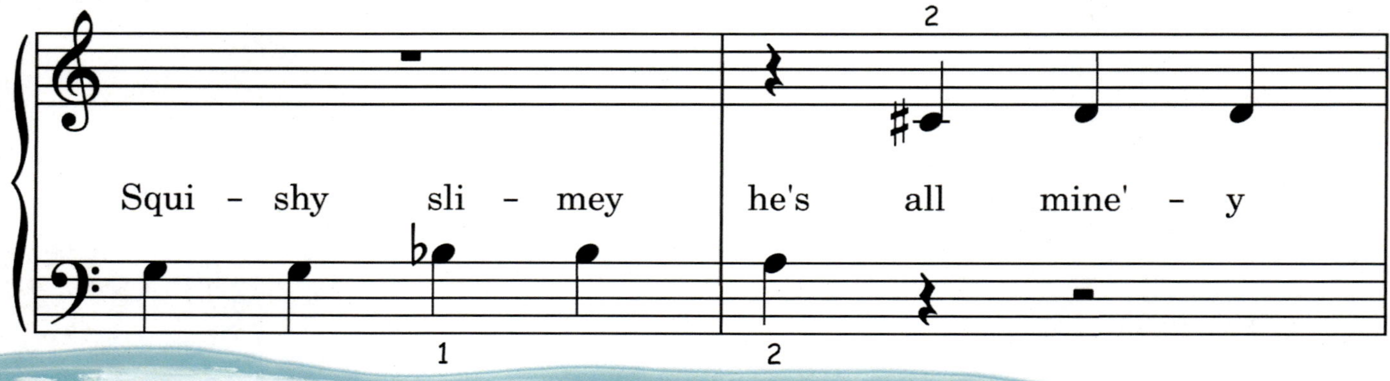

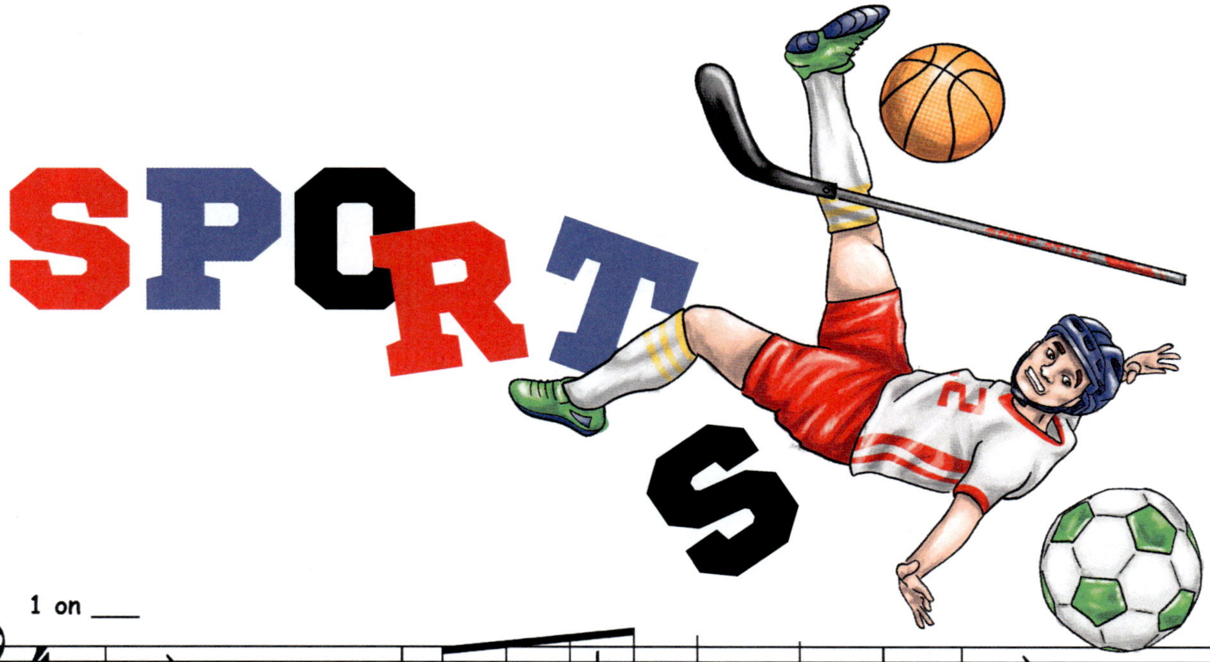

SPORTS

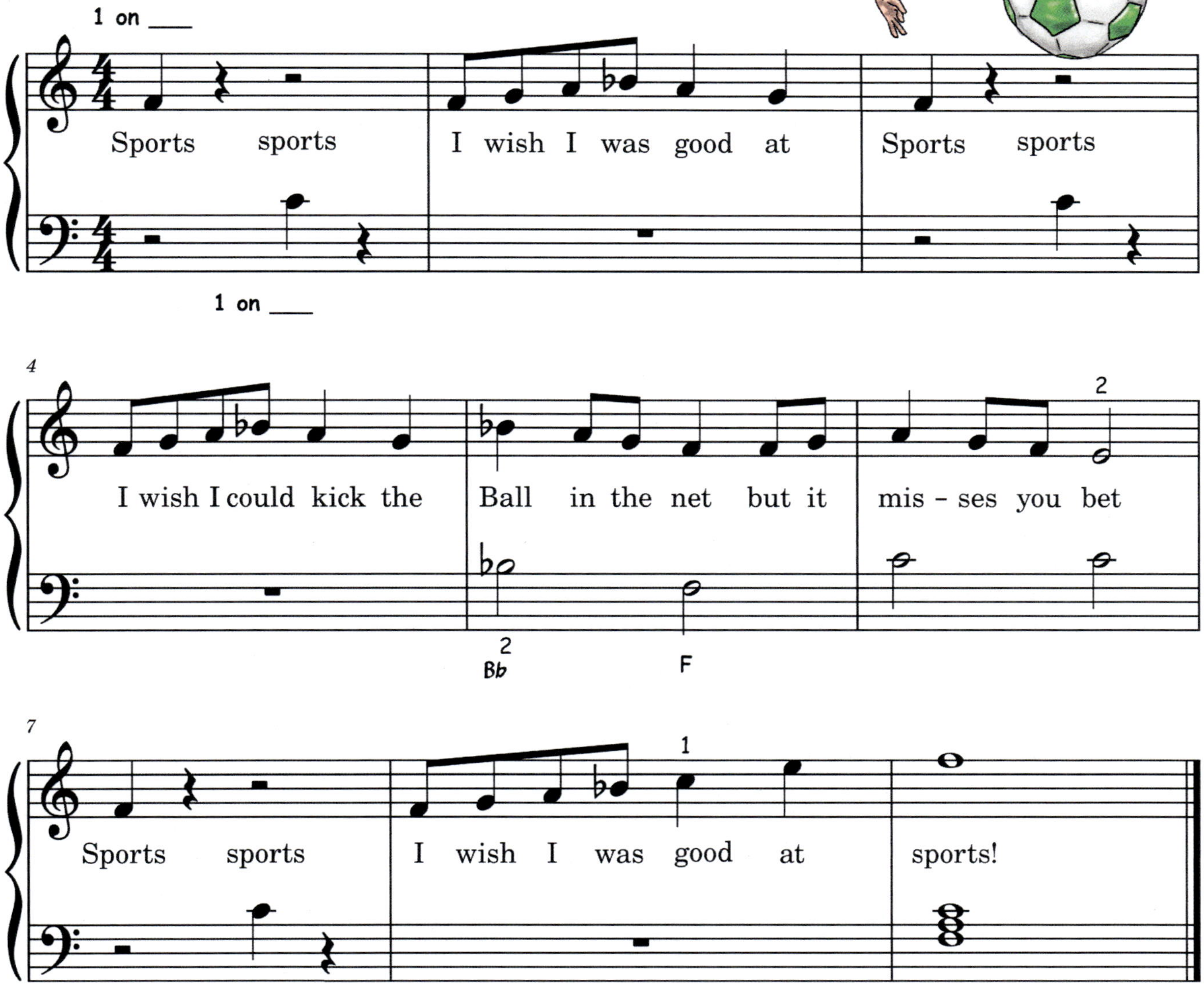

1 on ___
Sports sports
I wish I was good at
Sports sports
1 on ___
I wish I could kick the
Ball in the net but it
mis - ses you bet
2
2
Bb
F
Sports sports
I wish I was good at
1
sports!

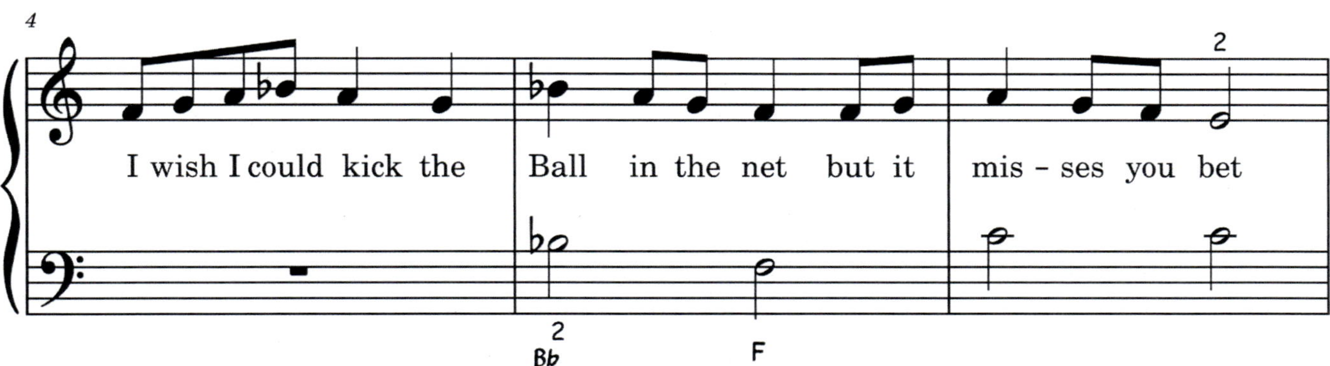

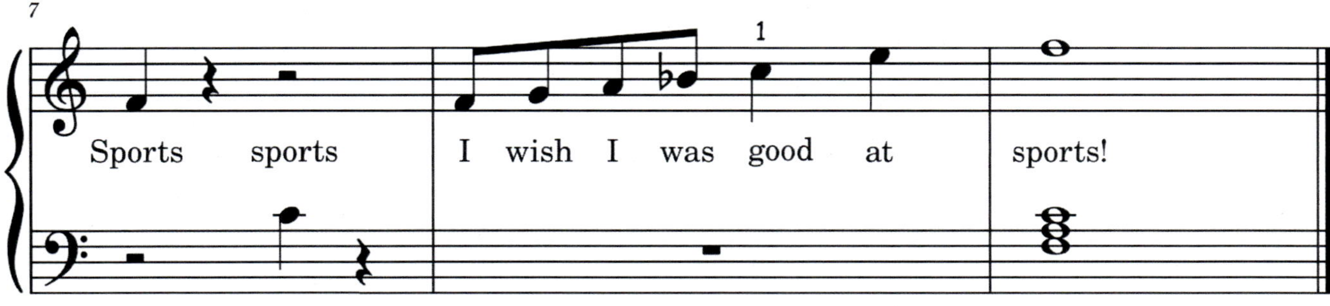

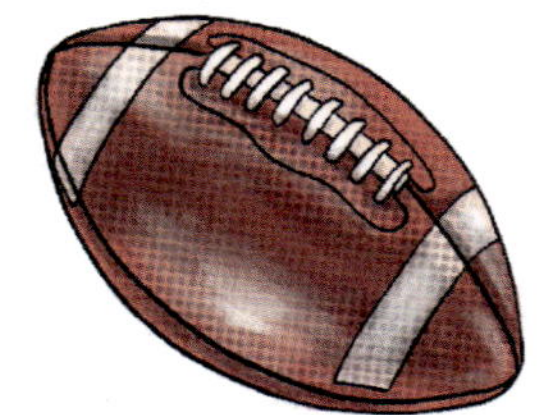

Little Frog

WARTISIOUS TOADICUS
JUMPIFICUS FROGINIUM
Lit - tle frog you are an am - phi - bi an Not a
1 on ____
LH Cross over RH
toad but a frog Toads are Frogs but it's weir der
2 1
than that Not all frogs are toads

Dynamics

Dynamics are about how loudly you play!

pp	=	pianissimo	=	very quiet
p	=	piano	=	quiet
mp	=	mezzo piano	=	medium quiet
mf	=	mezzo forte	=	medium loud
f	=	forte	=	loud
ff	=	fortissimo	=	very loud

SHARK!
1 on ___
p
Is that a shark?
Think I see a fin
3 on ___

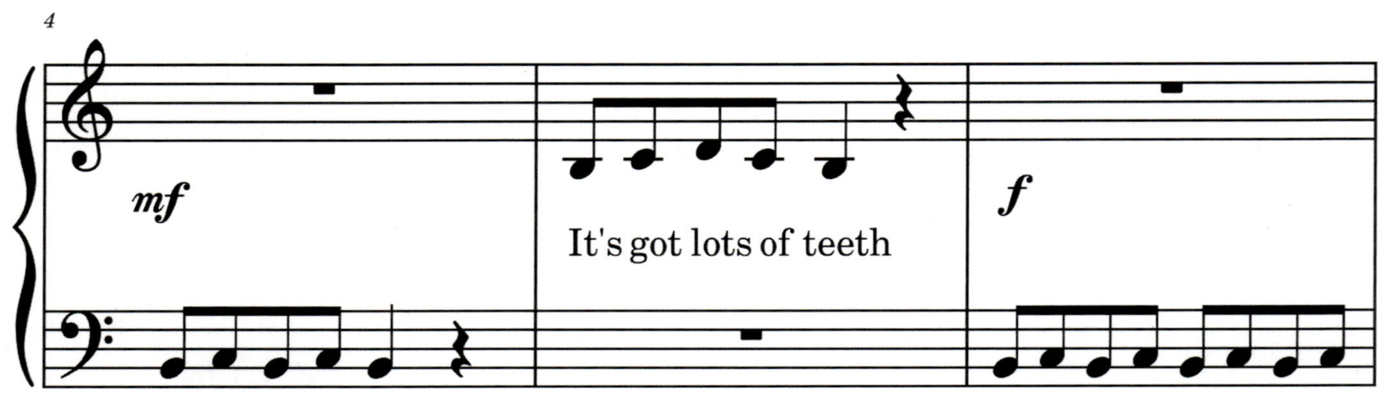
4
mf
It's got lots of teeth
f

7
p
Glad I'm in a pool!
(fewf)

Tip-toe STOMP
5 on ___
f
p
Tip-toe tip-toe
Tip-toe tip-toe Stomp!
5 on ___
3
A
p This part is qui - et
qui - et as a mouse
5
f This part is loud like a
rhi - no in the house
7
f
p Tip-toe tip-toe
Tip-toe tip-toe Stomp!

Monkey Monkey
1 on ___
f Mon-key Mon-key
Mon-key Mon-key
G
C
5 on ___
p I just want to eat ba - na - nas
f Mon-key mon-key
Mon-key mon-key
p I just want to swing on bran - ches

Creepy Crawly Spider
1 on ___
A
f
Cree-py craw-ly spi - der
build-ing a big web
5 on ___
Fine
It's got lots of eye - balls
on its lit - tle head
p
Watch out! Watch out!
Cree-py craw-ly Cree-py craw-ly
D.C. al Fine
(go back to beginning
play till you hit 'Fine')
Watch out! Watch out!
Watch out for the
69

Cheese!

5 on ___
Cheese cheese cheese cheese
Ched-dar Moz-za-rel - la
C
1
1 on ___
①
Gou-da and Ha-var - ti
⑤
①
Pro-vo-lone and Fe - ta
⑤
3
2
1
These are kinds of cheese I like to
eat!
4
1
5
finger replace
Replace your 4th with your thumb on same note

Wizard Guy
1 on ____
Hel-lo mis-ter wi - zard will you cast a ma-gic spell
2 on ____
Hel - lo mis - ter wi - zard guy
will you make my home-work fly?
Fly a
waaaa - aaa - aa - aa - aa - aa - aaay

tornado
1 on ___
f
A
5 on ___
p
f

Fathoms Deep

SUPERHERO

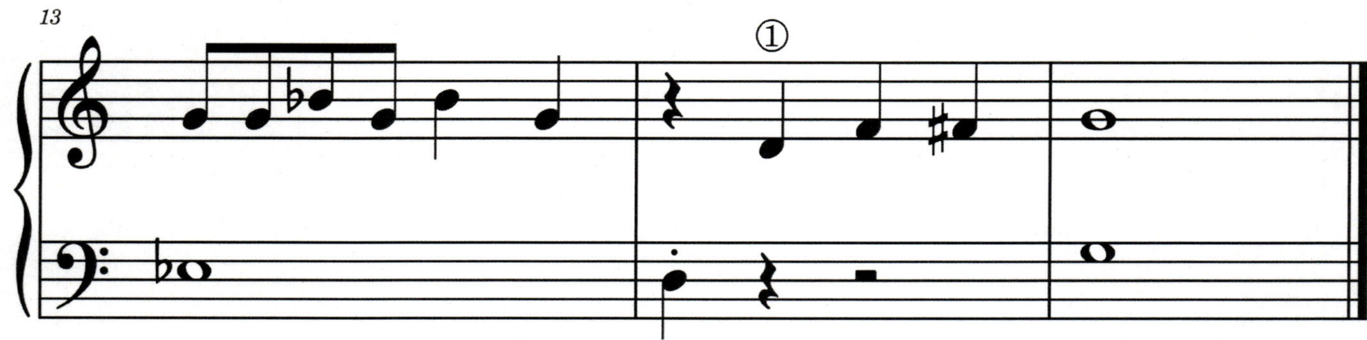

Save Game?

Do not close book while saving is in progress.

Planets
MERCURY
VENUS
EARTH
MARS
3 on ___
___ Chord
Can you name the pla - nets in the so - lar sys - tem
I bet you can't name them in a ro - oo - w
Mer - cu - ry and Ve - nus and then Earth and Mars
Ju - pi - ter and Sa - turn Ur - a - nus and Nep - tune

9
①
1
These are all the pla - nets that I know

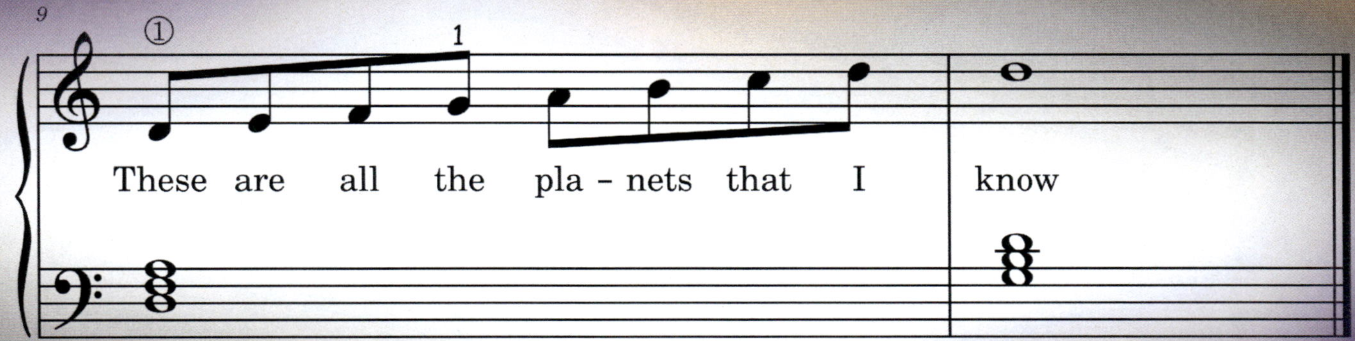

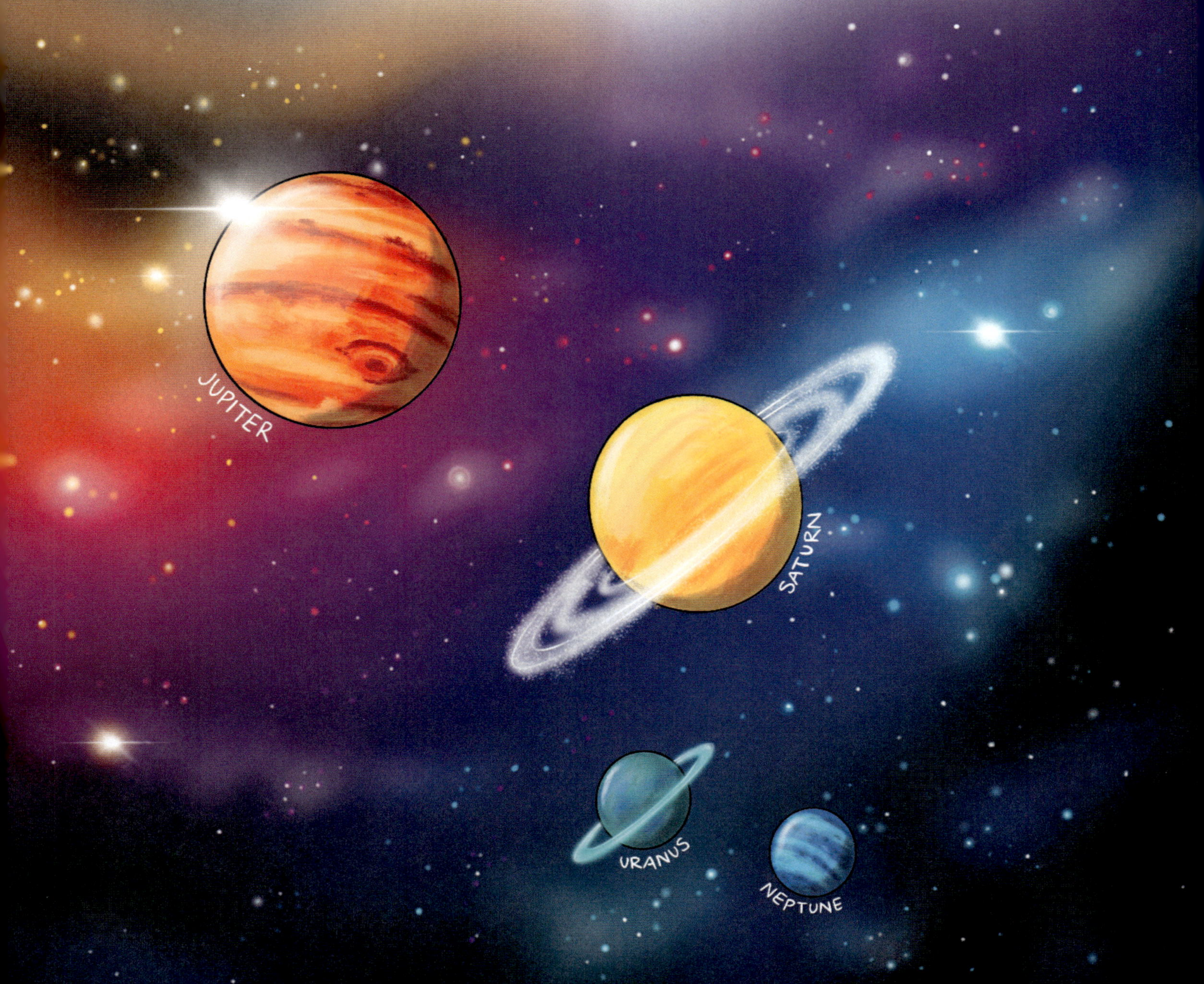
JUPITER
SATURN
URANUS
NEPTUNE

Boss Fight I

Infernal Swamp Basilisk

Minuet in G

Composed by Bach
Arranged by James AG

rit. stands for ritardando
this means slow down

The A-G
Piano Book Series

About Us!

James Atin-Godden

James is a composer, teacher, and producer originally from the small town of Kingsville, Ontario. Since graduating from York University with a music degree, James has gone on to participate in a huge variety of musical endeavours. He has produced tracks and albums for various artists, toured Canada with bands, wrote music for various mediums, and taught many piano lessons. He has also written this book series. He's now living in the present tense. He's currently probably on his couch playing video games, or maybe practicing.

Meredith Wolting

Meredith is a painter, graphic designer, and singer who would have practiced piano more if she'd had a colourful book like this. She loves musical theatre, and since studying set and costume design at York University, she has been busy building dragons, painting forests, and creating castles to come alive on the stage. Meredith also paints murals for homes, leads workshops for young artists, and sings show tunes for just about anyone.

Made in the USA
Monee, IL
24 August 2022